Zechariah

Zechariah

The Gift of Vision

Ronald B. Gifford

CHRISTIAN PUBLICATIONS, INC.
CAMP HILL, PENNSYLVANIA

Christian Publications, Inc.
3825 Hartzdale Drive, Camp Hill, PA 17011
www.cpi-horizon.com

Faithful, biblical publishing since 1883

ISBN: 0-87509-629-8

Printed in the
United States of America

98 99 00 01 02 5 4 3 2 1

Contents

To Joan,

fellow-pilgrim,
life-long friend,
mother of my children,
partner in ministry,
impatient with pretensions,
never satisfied with the shallow,
profound in prayer,
attuned to the voice . . .

May "the gift of vision" be yours.

Zechariah:

The Gift of Vision

The times were cruel,
the people were grimly surviving,
just hanging on, almost without hope.

Then the Lord gave to His people
the gift of vision,
the ability to see beyond immediate realities . . .
first, the vision to see things the way
they really are (chapters 1-6),
then, vision to see things the way they
ought to be (chapters 7-8),
finally, vision to see the way things are
going to be one day (chapters 9-14) . . .
with a dramatic finish!

Let's seek the Lord
to give us this gift of vision too.

Introduction

The Hope of Revival and the Revival of Hope

Zechariah 1:1-6

In the eighth month of the second year of Darius, the word of the Lord *came to the prophet Zechariah son of Berekiah, the son of Iddo:*

"The Lord *was very angry with your forefathers. Therefore tell the people: This is what the* Lord *Almighty says: 'Return to me,' declares the* Lord *Almighty, 'and I will return to you,' says the* Lord *Almighty. Do not be like your forefathers, to whom the earlier prophets proclaimed: This is what the* Lord *Almighty says: 'Turn from your evil ways and your evil practices.' But they would not listen or pay attention to me, declares the* Lord*. Where are your forefathers now? And the prophets, do they live forever? But did not my words and my decrees, which I commanded my servants the prophets, overtake your forefathers?*

"Then they repented and said, 'The Lord *Almighty has done to us what our ways and practices deserve, just as he determined to do.' "*

There are times in our lives and in the life of the Church when we need to hear from God again.

Zechariah's first message had the ring and the force of the prophets from an earlier age. It could be captured in nine words that were both hard and hopeful: "Return to me . . . and I will return to you." The book of this prophet's visions and messages is a compact revival series for discouraged people, with themes that are as poignant and penetrating in our century and in our discouragements as they were in his. His spiritually penetrating book needs to be recovered from obscurity and heard again.

Understanding Judah's story is the first key to understanding the book of Zechariah.[1] The people of Judah were preoccupied with survival, having been reduced by Babylon to a grim, hardscrabble existence yielding little room for hope.

Dispersion was king Nebuchadnezzar's crushing answer to dissent in his emerging empire. Before he was done, the land of Judah was empty and lying in ruin, enjoying the sabbath rest that was its due every seventh year (Exodus 23:11), but which very likely had never been observed.

Daniel was taken to Babylon with the first group of captives (Daniel 1:1-6) and lived to see Cyrus of Persia take over the city of Babylon one October night sixty-seven years later (Daniel 5). Then, taking his cue from the prophecy of Jeremiah, he began to pray for a return to the land of his birth (9:1-19).

With that prayer the empire's policy changed. Rather than try to extinguish the Jewish religion and sense of national identity, Cyrus encouraged it in order to win their loyalty and gratitude. He even gave them funds and permission to return to Jerusalem to build a temple (Ezra 1).[2] Their longings for home, so plaintively sung in the exile psalm, "By the rivers of Babylon we sat and wept when we remembered Zion" (Psalm 137:1), abruptly emerged into a real opportunity to return.

The call went out to those who would uproot and stake the claim of a scattered nation on its home soil. Fifty thousand of the sons of Judah returned to Jerusalem under the leadership of Zerubbabel, grandson of Jehoiachin, the man who would have been their king if there were still a kingdom.[3] He stood as a leader among them, a prince of the house of David, heir to a throne that no longer existed—and he led them back, along with a high priest by the auspicious name of Joshua (Ezra 3:2; Zechariah 3).

The first thing on the agenda for the returning exiles was to begin construction of a temple in the rubble of what had been the beautiful and sacred city of Jerusalem. But the project soon bogged down. The difficulty of starting life from scratch was too discouraging and the harassment of their neighbors was a constant grief. After two years of pain and strain, the construction came to a halt. It seemed that the promises of Isaiah that had nursed the people for all those years in Babylon[4] were not going to be fulfilled, or at least not in their lifetime. Unable to sense God's presence, they walked away from the temple project to look after the basic needs of life in an unyielding environment. The foundation stones of a new temple lay bare for fourteen years while the nation-builders did their best to bring some security into their miserable lives (Haggai 1:1-15). Then two prophets emerged, preaching a real revival—the kind we all need.

A young mother recently overheard her three-year-old daughter scolding one of her dolls. "You were making noise in church. That was bad! You woke up all those other people!" Perhaps that isn't so bad. Sometimes God wakes us up with a very pointed prophetic message.

Haggai was the first preacher to bring a wake-up call to Judah. He was an old man who, judging by the sermon outlines he left us, had probably seen the original temple. His message was simple. He said, "Your lives are in ruin because you left the house of God in ruin. If you step out and resume building that temple, the Lord says, 'I will bless you again' " (see 2:1-9). There was a dramatic response. Within days the people organized and were building. And soon after the construction resumed, Zechariah, the younger man in the prophetic duo, stepped up with this challenge: "While the building project is reviving, let's have a spiritual revival too." His book of messages is packed with hope.

They had answered the summons to return to the land. Now there was another call to return—a more profound and prophetically forceful summons, offering again both challenge and hope: "Return to *me* . . . and I will return to you" (Zechariah 1:3, emphasis added). For them it was a timely message. But it is also a timeless message, reaching across the centuries to other generations of God's people whose dreams have drained away into hopelessness. The message of Zechariah has a remarkable poignancy and lasting force.

After the opening challenge, Zechariah communicates his vision of the way things really are (chapters

1-6). There are realities that we cannot discern without the Lord's gift of vision. The second section of the book is a vision of the way things ought to be (chapters 7-8). Once again our sight is corrected, with an explanation of judgment and a penetrating presentation of ten promises of God. The third section is a vision of what will be one day (chapters 9-14). Sagging hope is restored with fresh insight into the future that the Lord has prepared for us all. With God giving His people these visions of greater realities, hope is breathed into our pressure-filled existence, and hopelessness yields to vision. The messages of Zechariah offer the hope of revival and the revival of hope for discouraged people.

"In the eighth month of the second year of Darius, the word of the LORD came to the prophet Zechariah son of Berekiah, the son of Iddo" (1:1).

The years of Jewish history were at one time based upon the regnal year of the descendant of David sitting on the throne. ("In the twenty-third year of Joash son of Ahaziah king of Judah . . ." [2 Kings 13:1], or "In the fourteenth year of King Hezekiah's reign . . ." [18:13]). Perhaps they could still have done that, though they had no reigning king. They still had a son of David as their leader. They could have said that it was "the eighth month of the sixteenth year after the return of Zerubbabel." But though they were back in their land, and though they were led by a prince of David's family, there was an awareness among them that these were the times of the Gentiles. They used a Gentile calendar, pushing into the unforeseeable future any hope of Isaiah's days-of-gold promises being fulfilled.

In our calendar, the eighth month of the second year of Darius would be November 520 B.C. Because we have such a specific date, we know what was happening in their world. The empire was in turmoil. Cyrus the Persian took over the Median Empire in 550. He conquered Babylon in 539 and announced his policy of repatriation in 538. Zerubbabel and Joshua led a return of exiles in 537, laying the foundation of the second temple in the spring of 536, seventy years after the first deportation, as Jeremiah had predicted. Cyrus was then replaced by his son Cambyses, who was not at all sympathetic to the Jews. More than that, he conquered Egypt, so that there was no hope for the Jews to escape from the sovereignty of the massive and hostile Persian Empire. The folks in Judah were giving up hope that God was going to rescue them any time soon. Everything was going the wrong way. They had every reason in the world to leave their building project for another day.

In 522 B.C. Cambyses himself was in Palestine. He was on his way back from a military campaign in Egypt when he heard that there had been a massive coup in Babylon. In fact, many of the royal family and the officers of the army had joined the leaders of the insurrection. Perceiving the situation to be beyond reclaiming, Cambyses committed suicide. It was a dynamic moment in history when the Persian Empire was up for grabs.

There was a young officer in Cambyses' entourage named Darius. He was a member of the royal family by a collateral line and he immediately claimed the throne. Gathering together as much of the army as he could, he went back to Babylon to enter into the struggle for the succession. For several months, every Persian province from the Aegean Sea to the eastern reaches of Iran was in revolt—Darius had a fight on his hands. It was in this time of uncertainty that Haggai stood up among his people and talked about the Lord shaking the nations (Haggai 2:6-7). It was a moment of hope—hope that the power of the evil empire had been broken. With the Persian master looking less formidable, people dared to hope again, and they resumed work on the temple.

Then Zechariah stood up before the people with a further word of hope that if they returned to the Lord, they would find Him returning to them.

Something new was happening. The temple construction was underway. Once again God was speaking through His old prophet, whose pointed challenge came with a new promise. Then the first message of this younger prophet came with a similar mix—including hope and a distressing jab. "Didn't you learn anything from our national tragedy? Just sixty-six years ago, our nation was finally crushed and our city was leveled by Nebuchadnezzar. It is only because of the mercy of God that we didn't disappear as a recognizable people." The message that the Lord gave the prophet to preach was not new. It was, "Return to me."

Returning to God was a major theme in the preaching of Hosea, whose wayward wife had made the appeal the more anguishing. Returning was a major theme in the preaching of Jeremiah, whose angst was intensified by his vision of what would happen if they did not.

"You have heard this before," Zechariah reminded them. "You need to *return* because the direction you have chosen is away from God. 'Return to me,' says the Lord Almighty."

Israel's story line may be different from ours. But the story, theirs or ours, is always the important context for God's message. The moments of opportunity in our lives are not always uncertain circumstances like theirs. Sometimes tragedies and failures force us to consider where we have been going with such life-consuming intensity. But the challenge and invitation ring with a still-current thrust. It is a "U-turn" message that some of us need to hear. When our lives are spent following our own goals, the Lord sends a messenger to warn us that we must reverse our direction and make Him the goal of our lives. Although it is hard to be told that we are wrong, sometimes we need to hear it.

My wife and I have friends who decided to drive from the comfortable climate of White Rock, British Columbia to the deep freeze of Winnipeg on the Canadian prairies for Christmas one year. John and Elsie set out with their three teenage daughters to make the trip of 1,450 miles across the ranges of Rocky Mountains and the seemingly limitless stretch of open prairie—at a time of year when dangerous weather can be expected.

The Trans-Canada Highway is clearly marked with green signs the shape of a maple leaf and a prominent Number 1. They simply had to get on the big road less than ten miles from their home and follow it through three-and-a-half provinces for twenty-five hours! They drove all night through the mountains, and then across the Alberta prairies the next day, stopping for supper in Medicine Hat at a junction with another highway. It was getting dark as they got back into their car, each one finding a pillow and nestling down while their daughter Lori took her turn at the wheel. John woke up a couple of hours later, a little disoriented from his sleep and confused by the unfamiliar landmarks. He wasn't sure of his sense of direction until a large sign emerged that said, "Welcome to Lethbridge." They were on the wrong road! For 100 miles they had been traveling west instead of east! Lori could only weakly offer, "I didn't think this was familiar."

Imagine the feeling. You are under pressure to get to your destination and you don't have any time to waste. What an awful feeling to recognize that you have been on the wrong road. What a waste of time! There is nothing you can do but turn around and drive that same road the other way. The voice of the prophet cried, "You have been going the wrong way, folks. And you know where that leads because you have lived with the results of your grandparents and your parents making that same decision. Don't make that mistake! Turn around now and return to Me."

The message of Jeremiah was, "You are on the wrong road and it is too late—judgment is inevitable." The message of Zechariah is much more hopeful. He says, "Return to Me, declares the Lord Almighty, because I want to return to you."

The language here is strikingly personal. This is not "Return to righteous living." It is not "Return to the building project." This is not even "Return to the blessings I have promised you." This is "Return to *Me*. Turn your life around and point it in My direction. Make the pursuit of God the goal of your life and make everything else secondary. And 'you will seek me and find me when you seek me with all your heart' " (Jeremiah 29:13). The first word of hope for this discouraged people is a warm invitation to come back to the Lord—to learn from their history and let the revival of their building project become a spiritual revival, too.

The challenge is, "Return to me." The promise is, "I will return to you." The challenge is the message of the first six verses. The promise is the message of the next six chapters. We still need both. God interrupted the history of His people with an opportunity, a challenge, an invitation and a promise. He still does. These opening verses of Zechariah summon us to leave the shallows of a spirituality that is content with little and invite us to walk into the deeper water of understanding and knowing God, where His blessing is to be found again.

Discussion Questions for Further Study

1. What pursuits can take us away from the Lord?
2. In what ways are we like our forefathers? What can we learn from the mistakes of those who have gone before us?
3. What in your personal circumstances might God be using to call you back to Himself?
4. Recall some of God's promises that await those who return to Him with all their heart.

Endnotes

[1] The story as presented here and throughout the book has been gathered from the details in working commentaries and other resources listed in the bibliography.

[2] His successor, Darius Hystaspes, gave an insight into the Persian policy when he reinforced Cyrus' decree and added, "The expenses . . . are to be fully paid out of the royal treasury . . . so that they may offer sacrifices pleasing to the God of heaven and pray for the well-being of the king and his sons" (Ezra 6:8-10).

[3] Matthew 1:12. Jeconiah was another name for Jehoiachin.

[4] After thirty-nine chapters of very challenging messages, Isaiah 40-66 is a collection of his promise themes, encouragement for the remnant who would survive the judgment that was sure to come.

Part 1

The Way Things Really Are

1

The Lord Is in Control

Zechariah 1:7-21

On the twenty-fourth day of the eleventh month, the month of Shebat, in the second year of Darius, the word of the Lord *came to the prophet Zechariah son of Berekiah, the son of Iddo.*

During the night I had a vision—and there before me was a man riding a red horse! He was standing among the myrtle trees in a ravine. Behind him were red, brown and white horses.

I asked, "What are these, my lord?"

The angel who was talking with me answered, "I will show you what they are."

Then the man standing among the myrtle trees explained, "They are the ones the Lord *has sent to go throughout the earth."*

And they reported to the angel of the Lord*, who was standing among the myrtle trees, "We have gone throughout the earth and found the whole world at rest and in peace."*

Then the angel of the Lord *said, "*Lord *Almighty, how long will you withhold mercy from Jerusalem and from the towns of Judah, which you have been angry* *with these seventy years?" So the LORD spoke kind and comforting words to the angel who talked with me.*

Then the angel who was speaking to me said, "Proclaim this word: This is what the LORD Almighty says: 'I am very jealous for Jerusalem and Zion, but I am very angry with the nations that feel secure. I was only a little angry, but they added to the calamity.'

"Therefore, this is what the LORD says, 'I will return to Jerusalem with mercy, and there my house will be rebuilt. And the measuring line will be stretched out over Jerusalem,' declares the LORD Almighty.

"Proclaim further: This is what the LORD Almighty says: 'My towns will again overflow with prosperity, and the LORD will again comfort Zion and choose Jerusalem.' "

Then I looked up—and there before me were four horns! I asked the angel who was speaking to me, "What are these?"

He answered me, "These are the horns that scattered Judah, Israel and Jerusalem."

Then the LORD showed me four craftsmen. I asked, "What are these coming to do?"

He answered, "These are the horns that scattered Judah so that no one could raise his head, but the craftsmen have come to terrify them and throw down these horns of the nations who lifted up their horns against the land of Judah to scatter its people."

It was the twenty-fourth day of Shebat, three months later. On our calendar it was February 15, 519 B.C. A lot had happened in three months. With remarkable skill and in short order, Darius had arrived in Babylon and put down all of the challenges to his succession. That news was discouraging, even faith-crushing, for the Jewish people. They had hoped that the Lord was shaking the nations and that, with the dismemberment of the Persian Empire, they would soon be a free people again. But the regime was still strongly intact under a new tyrant. The window of optimism in the international news was slammed shut and bolted tight so fast that their discouragement was deeper for having been allowed the lift of a little hope. It must be clear that our hope has to turn on something other than current events.

With these new developments, the prophet stood before the Jews again with another word from "the LORD Almighty." Five times in his first short message he had reminded them of this strong name of God. In the first vision scene that follows, their covenant God is again identified as the one who is "Almighty." The repetition is obviously emphatic. "No matter what may be the news, this is the character of the God that you serve, and you need to hear from Him, especially now. You need to see a new vision of Him." And that is what He gave them.

"During the night I had a vision—and there before me was a man riding a red horse!" (1:8) The scenes of this remarkable prophetic experience go on for six chapters. We quickly sense that this vision is not just a colorful dream of tangled metaphors caused by too much anxiety or prophetic enthusiasm. These are not just elaborate figures of speech or poetic devices that seek to describe spiritual realities. They are pictures of what the Lord is doing, what He is thinking, what He is feeling and what He is planning to do. What

Zechariah saw was a reality that is always there, though we are only occasionally aware of it.

Vision is a gift that God wants to give to His people through the book of Zechariah. Vision penetrates outward appearances. Vision is insight into another reality that lies behind the one that we commonly see. God's gift of vision is a description of the way things really are. So often discouragement tricks us into believing that our circumstances are the most real phenomena in the universe, when in fact they are just the most immediate.

It is important to keep all the characters in the picture straight. There is a dominant figure in this first scene that must be identified right away. He appears as a man riding a red horse and is soon called "the Angel of the LORD." That is a proper name, and he is a figure that appears at critical moments in the Old Testament.[1] He is special in the cosmology of the universe; many believe Him to be the Son of God appearing among the people of God before He was incarnate as a man known as Jesus. The first scene is a vision of the Lord.

The second figure to note is the interpretive angel standing beside Zechariah. We will see him and rely on his guidance as we are shown all the scenes of the vision. He is the one who says to the prophet, "Let me show you what this is about."

The vision is the Lord's gift of encouragement to His prophet, and it comes from a place the national news cannot go. It is a tour through the ultimate reality of the spiritual world that is behind what we commonly see. The Lord wanted Zechariah to see what was happening on the other side concurrent with the discouraging developments in the news.

The Lord Knows (1:7-11)

"There before me was a man riding a red horse! He was standing among the myrtle trees in a ravine" (1:8).

The symbolism throughout the vision is rich, and it is likely that the symbols were more easily understood by Zechariah and his contemporaries than they are by us—though he did have to ask for an explanation.[2]

When we turn on our television and see a peacock logo, we know that we are watching NBC. Five connecting rings signify the Olympic Games. Great Britain is the lion, the United States is the eagle and Russia is the bear. The rising sun is the symbol of Japan, the maple leaf is the symbol of Canada, the cedar is the symbol of Lebanon. Similarly, the myrtle trees that grew all over Israel were so common that a popular name for Israel was "Hadassah"—the "Myrtle Tree."[3]

We are seeing in the vision that the nation of Israel is in a ravine. God's people were in a deep valley at this point in their national life. But dominant in the picture is the Angel of the Lord among the myrtle trees. The Lord was right there with them. He was in the land, and all of these riders are His servants who were patrolling the earth.

The Persian Empire was twice as large as the Babylonian Empire largely because of one innovation: pavement. They built roads everywhere. The empire was divided into 120 provinces with a satrap responsible for each one. Satraps had enormous power, but they could not imagine being independent of the empire because the king had eyes ev-erywhere. In fact, the secret service was popularly called "the King's eyes!" Nobody knew who they were, but there was a most efficient courier system that sent riders on horseback up and down those phenomenal new roads. Back in Babylon, the emperor would know everything that was going on within a matter of days.

What Zechariah was seeing is that God has a system like that too. We know that God knows everything—He doesn't need people on horseback to come and tell Him; but the vision is a graphic way for Him to say, "I know." It says more than that: just like Darius had special agents out there, the Lord has unseen agents abroad, too.

In the first chapter of Job, the Lord asked Satan, "Where have you been?" Satan replied, "I've been out patrolling the earth, going back and forth in it" (see 1:7). We shudder when we read that, because we know that it is real. And it is important for us to know that Satan is on the prowl—that is why his activity is described for us so graphically in Job. Now we are being shown something else that we need to see just as clearly. The Lord's agents are patrolling the earth too. They are in the land just as surely as the Lord is, just as surely as Satan is. The first scene in the vision is a picture of the Angel of the Lord among the people of Israel. He was with them in the valley of their experience, and His angelic servants were patrolling the earth.

They came back to report that the world was at rest and in peace. That may appear to us to be good news, but it prompted an anguished response from the Angel of the Lord. If the disruption in the evil empire was good news for the people of God, word of rest and peace meant that the Persian power was now so solidly in control everywhere that no effective opposition was possible.

The Lord Cares (1:12-15)

In verse 12 the man on the red horse expressed the distress of God's people. Can you imagine Jesus interceding for us? Here is a picture of it. When the news came in, the Angel of the Lord grieved, "LORD Almighty, how long will you withhold mercy from Jerusalem and from the towns of Judah, which you have been angry with these seventy years?" It felt like the Lord would indefinitely withhold His mercy from His people as He had for all this time.

Seventy years had passed between Nebuchadnezzar's first deportation of Jews to Babylon and the return of the first exiles to rebuild the temple. Now it was almost seventy years since the city and the temple had been completely destroyed. (Incidentally, the day that the new temple was dedicated was seventy years from the time the old temple was demolished.) Jeremiah's prophecy of seventy years' exile (29:10-14) was fulfilled twice. But seventy years of the Lord's displeasure was an almost crushing experience. The Angel of the Lord is expressing how they felt. This is a picture of Him entering into their feelings and praying for them.

Next we have a picture of the Lord speaking kind and comforting words to Zechariah's interpreter. "This is what the LORD Almighty says: 'I am very jealous for Jerusalem and Zion.' " Do you ever wonder what God feels? "I am very jealous . . . and I am very angry." He says, "I feel very deeply the suffering you have experienced. I authorized the difficult things that have happened to you. I was angry with you a little, but 'they added to the calamity.' The nations I used to punish you went much too far and I am very, very angry with them for what they did to you."

In one of the first glimpses we have of God, He is seeking out Adam and Eve in the garden. We do not read the story as it was intended to be understood if we picture God as the policeman coming to apprehend the disobedient and to punish them. He didn't have to come at all if His purpose was simply to judge. Rather, it is a scene full of tender care, with a clear description of the consequences to be sure, but also with the provision of garments of skin. They "heard the sound of the LORD God as he was walking in the garden in the cool of the day" (Genesis 3:8). We like to imagine that as part of their daily experience. He called out, "Where are you?" not because He didn't know, but because He wanted them to come to Him. This is not the cosmic cop walking His nightly beat; it is the brokenhearted Father looking for His lost children. Even this chapter of judgment is full of His care and mercy.

The Lord knows. The Lord cares. And He gave His prophet Zechariah a picture to show that to His people. He also said very clearly that this time of His displeasure would come to an end. His jealousy and His anger would soon emerge.

The Lord Will Return (1:16-17)

"I will return . . . my house will be rebuilt. . . . My towns will again overflow . . . the LORD will again comfort Zion and choose Jerusalem" (1:16-17).

When the power of Persia is re-established as never before, when the angelic couriers of the Lord report in to say that the reign of evil is thoroughly entrenched, when the angel of the Lord is interceding for God's people with a desperate cry, "How much longer, Lord?" And when all that you can see is most discouraging and hard—*that* is when you need a vision of what God feels and what He is about to do. "I am very jealous. . . . I am very angry. . . . I will return. . . . My house will be rebuilt. . . . My towns will again overflow. . . . The LORD will again comfort Zion" (1:14-17).

Walter Kaiser's title for this chapter is "Waiting in the Calm before the International Storm."[4] That's where we are too. The Lord knows, the Lord cares, the Lord will return, and when He comes it will be with specific judgment.

The Lord Will Bring Judgment (1:18-21)

"Then I looked up—and there before me were four horns! I asked the angel who was speaking to me, 'What are these?' " (1:18-19).

The horn was the symbol of brute power. The Rocky Mountain sheep crashing their heads together on the television commercials for pickup trucks are symbols of great strength. The wild moose and caribou and rhinoceros are fearsome because of their strength and their weapons. We bring back the horns of the ten-point buck as a trophy that symbolizes the triumph of our cunning over the mighty beast.

When Zechariah saw four horns, he was seeing power, and he was told that these were the powerful nations that had scattered Judah and Israel and Jerusalem. We know their story and we can trace successive devastations of the nation by their powerful neighbors: Egypt, Assyria, Babylon and Persia.[5] Trouble had come on God's people from every direction.

The message of encouragement for those discouraged people was that all the nations on every side would soon be terrified and thrown down by four skilled craftsmen. It was asking a lot to expect them to believe that. These people could see only the power of Persia, entrenched as it was. They could only believe this prophetic word by a sheer act of faith, because there were no hints on the horizon of who these craftsmen might be. But God was telling them that someday soon He would pour out His judgment on the nations.

When God shows us His jealous love for us and what He is about to do, we are called to return to Him, to rest patiently in His provident knowledge and care and to believe that He will do what He said He will do.

We have watched the fall of communism in recent years. That should make it easier for us to believe that these great predictions of entrenched powers collapsing before the plans of God are possible. I have a piece of the Berlin Wall sitting on my desk. Now we live in the "New World Disorder." We are uncertain where events will take us next. Some people are fearful. It is important for us to see all of that, to understand the times so that we can know what God's people should do (see 1 Chronicles 12:32).

But we must see this picture of God too. "My house will be rebuilt," He said. Three years later they dedicated that building. "The measuring line will be stretched out over Jerusalem," He said, meaning you will have to lay out construction plans to accommodate the large number of people who will come back to live in Jerusalem. Seventy-five years later, Nehemiah stretched out a measuring line that rebuilt the walls in a remarkable fifty-two days, and under his leadership Jerusalem was re-inhabited (Nehemiah 6:15; 11:1-2). Craftsmen had successfully overcome the opposition of the most powerful nation on earth.

The Babylonians and the Persians were strong by brute force, but when Alexander came along he was by far the most skillful general of the ancient world. He conquered mighty armies with small ones. When he died, his armies split his empire into four pieces, each led by one of his four great generals. Four remarkable military craftsmen had conquered the four horns of the ancient world in dramatic fashion.

What God says He will do, He will do. So do not be like your forefathers. "Return to me and I will return to you." Wait with confident expectation. Go to work on the temple, anticipating the end of the seventy years of the Lord's displeasure. Stand in awe of the terrific battle shaping up, confident of who is really in control. "Stand firm. Let nothing move you. Always give yourselves fully to the work of the Lord, because you know that your labor in the Lord is not in vain" (1 Corinthians 15:58).

Whatever your valley, the Lord knows and the Lord cares. Hold on to this word of hope: The Lord will return, and when He does He will surely and decisively make things right. He gives us the gift of vision so that He can give us a deeper confidence in Him.

Discussion Questions for Further Study

1. What do we already know about "God Almighty" that we need to see when we are in the valley of life's experience?
2. What pressing circumstances tend to dominate your life?
3. List your difficult recurring emotions. Read Hebrews 4:15. How does God feel about your emotions?

4. The vision didn't promise an immediate answer—the Jews were asked to believe God when the answer was nowhere in sight. What challenges your faith? What does God ask you to believe that there is little tangible evidence for now?
5. What discouraging circumstances will be instantly taken care of when the Lord returns?
6. What entrenched powers of evil in our world will someday collapse under the judgment of the Lord?

Endnotes

[1] Genesis 16:7-14; Exodus 13:21-22; cf. 14:19-20; Numbers 22:22; Joshua 5:14-6:2; Judges 2:1-5; 6:1-22; Judges 13; 1 Chronicles 21:14-22:1. There are other instances when God appears in human form but is not specifically identified as "the Angel of the Lord."

[2] One of the keys to understanding the vision of the first six chapters is fitting it into their story. The other is seeking to discern what the symbols meant to the people of Zechariah's generation.

[3] Walter C. Kaiser, Jr., *Micah-Malachi*, The Communicator's Commentary, vol. 21 (Dallas, TX: Word Books, 1992), 305.

[4] Ibid., 302.

[5] "Many, including Jerome and most patristic commentators, have interpreted the four horns to be Babylonians, Medo-Persians, Greeks and Romans" [Ibid., 310]. That may neatly coincide with the Daniel prophecies, but it seems that the angel was talking about the powers that had already scattered them, not the ones they were yet to face. Higginson suggests that "possibly the numeral is symbolic rather of danger 'on every side,' just as we speak of the 'four' points of the compass. The people of God are ever surrounded by a menacing world." [R.E. Higginson, *Zechariah*, The New Bible Commentary, 3rd ed. (Grand Rapids: Wm. B. Eerdmans, 1970), 790.]

2

The Lord Will Live among Us

Zechariah 2:1-13

Then I looked up—and there before me was a man with a measuring line in his hand! I asked, "Where are you going?"

He answered me, "To measure Jerusalem, to find out how wide and how long it is."

Then the angel who was speaking to me left, and another angel came to meet him and said to him: "Run, tell that young man, 'Jerusalem will be a city without walls because of the great number of men and livestock in it. And I myself will be a wall of fire around it,' declares the Lord*, 'and I will be its glory within.'*

"Come! Come! Flee from the land of the north," declares the Lord*, "for I have scattered you to the four winds of heaven," declares the* Lord*.*

"Come, O Zion! Escape, you who live in the Daughter of Babylon!" For this is what the Lord *Almighty says: "After he has honored me and has sent me against the nations that have plundered you—for whoever touches you touches the apple of his eye—I will surely raise my hand against them so that their*

slaves will plunder them. Then you will know that the Lord *Almighty has sent me.*

"Shout and be glad, O Daughter of Zion. For I am coming, and I will live among you," declares the Lord. *"Many nations will be joined with the* Lord *in that day and will become my people. I will live among you and you will know that the* Lord *Almighty has sent me to you. The* Lord *will inherit Judah as his portion in the holy land and will again choose Jerusalem. Be still before the* Lord, *all mankind, because he has roused himself from his holy dwelling."*

"While we are rebuilding the temple, let's make this a time of spiritual rebuilding and renewal, too." That is the major thrust of the book of Zechariah. His vision, a series of pictures of the spiritual world, reinforced the message.

The vision came to him in one night "on the twenty-fourth day of the eleventh month, the month of Shebat, in the second year of Darius" (1:7). What we read here is not a man's conviction about spiritual realities and the future that percolated in his soul before emerging in colorful literature. Rather, the eight scenes of this vision were simply revealed to Zechariah on February 15, 519 B.C. It was not a shadowy dream with confusing patterns but clear pictures that were so distinct that he could remember the conversations. Even with the help of the interpreting angel, we are stretched to understand this vision of the spiritual realm. But it is an exhilarating look at what is happening in another reality that is very close to us. The gift of vision is the ability to see beyond visible realities.

The vision was meant to be a boost for us, too. It helps us to visualize the good and evil forces that are behind everything else that we see—a world of angels, spiritual dynamics, Satan and the Lord Almighty. It helps us understand more clearly the visible world of hard circumstances, godless nations and cultural forces that rule with great power. We need to see that God is at work, especially when we are disappointed with Him.[1] Though evil seems thoroughly entrenched, the vision reveals lots of action behind the scenes and developments about to happen. By the second chapter of Zechariah, we discover that the vision extends right into the days in which you and I are living.

Here, then, is the third scene: "Then I looked up—and there before me was a man with a measuring line" (2:1). There follows a statement of his assignment, a message from the Lord about His plans for the city, and a Hebrew poem, or oracle, which develops the special message the angel delivered to Zechariah.

His Plans Are Bigger Than Your Measuring Tape (2:1-5)

First comes this encouraging word: God says His plans are bigger than the ruins of your life. It's like driving down the same road every morning past a big piece of property that has always been empty and strewn with rubble. Then one day you see men with tripods out in that field and others pounding in red-tagged stakes. It is a signal that something is about to happen there. Somebody is planning something.

Zechariah asked, "Where are you going with your equipment?" The answer came, "To measure Jerusalem to find out how wide and how long it is" (2:2).

At that point in history Jerusalem was a mound of rubble. Sixteen years earlier, 50,000 people had returned from the exile in Babylon to an empty land. They built homes for themselves in the towns of Judah, but they had not resettled Jerusalem. There was no Jerusalem! There was only a modest temple project surrounded by the debris of what had once been a great and beautiful city. Then in Zechariah's vision there's a man who has been sent to measure up that city's space. God was planning for reconstruction to begin. He wanted His people to see that He was making preparations. Imagine it! Their hope had stretched far enough for them to resume rebuilding the temple, but it wasn't going to stop with that. Haggai had brought a message from the Lord that from the day they laid the cornerstone of the temple, the blessings would begin (Haggai 2:18-22), and then Zechariah was given a vision of the entire city being rebuilt!

> Then the angel who was speaking to me [that is, the interpreting angel] left, and another angel came to meet him and said to him: "Run tell that young man [Zechariah], 'Jerusalem will be a city without walls because of the great number of men and livestock in it.' " (Zechariah 2:3-4)

In the ancient world there were no unwalled cities. He was saying, "The city is going to be so big, so many people will come to live here, that you will not be able to put a wall around it." Measuring up the site of the old city would be just the beginning. God says that His plans are bigger than your ruins. And you won't need a wall for protection, for the Lord said, "I myself will be a wall of fire around it" (2:5).

The next line would have resonated profoundly in the spirit of any of the descendants of Israel with a sense of their heritage. "And I will be its glory within." This is the return of the Shekinah, the return of "the Presence," the most dramatic of all of the rich promises in this compact message.

When the Hebrew people left Egypt, the Lord graphically demonstrated His presence with them by appearing in a special cloud that stayed with them wherever they went. Shaped like a pillar, it contained a flame of fire within, so that at night it looked like a "pillar of fire." That dense cloud and holy flame led them through all of their desert years. When they built the tabernacle—the simple but symbolically rich tent structure that was their portable temple—the pillar of cloud and fire came down upon it, visibly showing them God's dwelling right there in the middle of their camp (Exodus 40:34-38). The cloud of fire was a great source of encouragement for the Hebrew people.

On the day that Solomon dedicated the temple he had built, the cloud of the Lord's presence came down upon that costly and magnificent structure too. It was so dramatic that all of the elaborate ceremony had to be suspended because the presence of God was so intense (2 Chronicles 7:1-3). For hundreds of years the holy cloud stood above the temple.

But over time the Jewish community lost their sense of God's holiness. Jeremiah stood up in front of that temple one day and said, "You people think that because you have the temple of the Lord here, you need not fear God's judgment. You keep nattering on that 'the temple of the LORD, the temple of the LORD, the temple of the LORD is here.' I'm here to tell you that the temple won't protect you from what the Lord intends to bring upon you because of your wicked lives" (see Jeremiah 7:1-8). The people responded in such anger that they tried to kill the prophet! They could not imagine losing their birthright, the Lord's presence and blessing, the pillar of cloud and the Shekinah flame. But they did, and the day it left, nobody seemed to notice (Ezekiel 9-10).

It is hard for Americans to imagine losing the blessing and prosperity we have enjoyed for so long. We are a specially blessed nation, and we have a sense of God's hand in our national history, much like the Hebrew people did. But it seems we have decided, like they did, that we can avoid the results of our ignoring God, shunting Him off to a minor byway of our national life. We expect to avoid the results of our abandoning morality. Incredibly, we even expect to avoid the results of our spending thirty percent more than we collect every year. We are blind to the possibility that we too may lose the blessing of God.

Israel lost their blessing and they lost God's presence. When Nebuchadnezzar visited Jerusalem in 597 B.C., he deported the leadership and military people of the nation, expecting with that to eliminate any further rebellion against his newly imposed authority (2 Kings 24:14). Among them was Ezekiel, a priest who became God's man in Babylon. Six-and-a-half years later, Ezekiel was sitting in his home with the elders of Judah when a vision came upon him that transported him back to the temple grounds where he had served (Ezekiel 8-10). He could see clearly the idolatry in the north gate, he could see people in the inner court with their backs to the temple bowing down to the sun, and in the private chambers of the temple complex he saw the elders of Jerusalem offering incense, "each at the shrine of his own idol" (8:12). He saw exploitation, injustice and profiteering.

As his vision continued it became ominous. "The glory of the God of Israel went up from above the cherubim, where it had been, and moved to the threshold of the temple" (9:3). The Lord was about to leave, but not before His judgment was poured out upon them. What followed was most severe. Ezekiel saw an angel mark the forehead of everyone who was grieved by what was happening in the temple. Then angels of death went throughout the city killing all who did not bear that mark, beginning at the temple precincts, and slaughtering without pity "old men, young men and maidens, women and children" (9:6). "Then the glory of the LORD departed from over the threshold of the temple" (10:18), and it went out of the city and over the mountain to the east.

This vision of God's impending judgment was so harsh that Pelatiah ben-Benaiah, one of the elders sitting there with Ezekiel, simply could not bear it, and he died (11:13). The day came when news arrived that the temple and the entire city had been completely destroyed (33:21)—it was an overwhelming tragedy. But at the heart of it was something more tragic yet. The loss of God's presence could not be remedied by a return to the land and a temple rebuilding project. The Shekinah was gone.

Almost seventy years later, after a long opportunity for the people to consider their history, Zechariah came to them with a call to return to the Lord, bringing His promise that He would return to them. In response, they began to rebuild the temple. But it was a basic block structure where there once had been marble and gold. It was almost too simple to be a real temple, and the few who were old enough to remember the splendor of Solomon's edifice celebrated this new beginning with some sadness (Haggai 2:3). But of greater importance, the building wasn't of much value without "the Presence."

Now the words of the Lord would ring out with compelling force—the general promise of the prophet became a specific prediction. The most precious lines in this third scene of the vision are these: " 'I myself will be a wall of fire around it,' declares the LORD, 'and I will be its glory within' " (Zechariah 2:5). The Shekinah would return!

The Lord intervened in the events of the times to deliver His people from their oppressors and to resettle them in their own land. He had begun a new work. Their work was the beginning of much grander things that God had in mind. The temple and the city would be rebuilt. His great plans gave meaning to their simple project and their hard service. It was important for them to see Him in the land, involved with them and about to do some dramatic things. The nations that had crushed them would be overthrown. Jerusalem would be rebuilt in greater dimensions than they would have dreamed. It was all very encouraging. Building was invigorating, the plans were exciting, the promise of renewed prosperity gave them a lift. But most important, at the center of this new work was God's intention to live among them again. The challenge for them, and the challenge for us, is to agree that we will never be satisfied with anything less.

The One the Lord Will Send (2:6-13)

The two-stanza messianic poem that follows explores what it will be like when the Lord returns. The prophetic promise of deliverance that had nursed God's people for generations emerged into a hope for a Deliverer as their focus sharpened. Fed by prophetic encouragement, there was a longing for a strong leader to arise—a larger-than-life figure, like Isaiah's "Servant of Yahweh" (Isaiah 49-53) and Daniel's "Son of Man" (Daniel 7:13-14). The "Angel of the Lord" who appeared in the first scene of the vision was familiar to them from their stories of Joshua, Gideon and others—a supernatural being who came to them at points of special need in their history.[2] Now the promise of the Lord's return depicts one like Him who is honored by the Lord and who will be sent against the nations that have plundered His people.

The poem also depicts the messianic day. "Many nations will be joined with the LORD in that day" (Zechariah 2:11). It is the "Day of the LORD." The prophets Joel, Amos, Isaiah and Zephaniah had already developed that theme extensively.[3] Since the loss of their national independence, God's people had been living in "the times of the Gentiles," as Jesus noted in Luke 21:24. But the nations and cultures that reign with flawed and evil people in charge will have their day, and then will come "the Day of the Lord." With that, people from "many nations . . . will become my people" (Zechariah 2:11). Not only was the Lord's intention for their city larger than they could have planned, but His purpose for drawing people to Himself was larger than their national aspirations.

The poetic language here fills in the colorful details of the promises of verses 4 and 5. God's people are called to return to the land, God's Messiah is presented with honor, God's punishment comes to the nations and God's people receive the One He has sent.

The second stanza (2:10-13) offers reasons to shout and reasons to stand silent in awe. The Lord is coming to live among you. Many nations will become His people. The Jewish people will receive Him. Jerusalem and Judah will again be His chosen.

Prophecy is history written in advance. Do you sense how the pieces are being assembled now on the world stage in our time for this ancient plan to be enacted in our history? "Come back to the land, My people." The return of the Jews to the land in the last 100 years is a striking literal fulfillment of this prophecy and others. They have come out of the pogroms of the tsars and the tyranny of the communists. Then they staggered out of the ashes of the Holocaust. With the War of Independence in 1948, most of the Jews of Syria came to Israel. When a Marxist government came to power in Yemen, all the Jewish people there moved within weeks to Israel. Early in this decade we have seen half a million finally released from the former Soviet states. Out of the turmoil of Ethiopia thousands of black-skinned Jews who had lived there for millennia were airlifted to Israel. The Israeli government has insisted that they need more space for all of these new citizens. The question in Israel was,

"Where are we going to put all of these people?" The city is too big, they say, to build the old wall around it any more. The return of the Jews is a phenomenon that signals the Day of the Lord.

The Jews have always been God's special people. In their desert experience, "He shielded [them] and cared for [them]; he guarded [them] as the apple of his eye" (Deuteronomy 32:10).[4] Now even though they are "plundered," the Lord's covenant love is still in effect.[5]

In her book *The Hiding Place*, Corrie ten Boom describes the horror of Nazi occupation in Holland during the Second World War. She includes this poignant memory:

> One day as Father and I were returning from our walk we found the Grote Markt cordoned off by a double ring of police and soldiers. A truck was parked in front of the fish mart; into the back were climbing men, women, and children, all wearing the yellow star. There was no reason we could see why this particular place at this particular time had been chosen.
>
> "Father! Those poor people!" I cried.
>
> The police line opened, the truck moved through. We watched till it turned the corner.
>
> "Those poor people," Father echoed. But to my surprise I saw that he was looking at the soldiers now forming into ranks to march away. "I pity the poor Germans, Corrie. They have touched the apple of God's eye."[6]

God's promise to Abraham and his descendants was unconditional, "God's gifts and his call are irrevocable"

(Romans 11:29). "If we are faithless, he will remain faithful, for he cannot disown himself" (2 Timothy 2:13). "Israel has experienced a hardening in part until the full number of the Gentiles has come in" (Romans 11:25). Jesus talked about "the times of the Gentiles" coming to an end (Luke 21:24). Here we read, "The LORD will inherit Judah as his portion in the holy land [the only place in the Bible where the land of Israel is called the 'holy land'] and will again choose Jerusalem" (Zechariah 2:12). This is a special city and these are special people. They were chosen once, they were set aside temporarily, but God will choose them again. He has not forgotten His promises.

The Lord is drawing His chosen people back to the land. Many nations are becoming His people as was predicted. There will come a day soon when the Messiah will appear again to be publicly honored and to save His people from those who would like to destroy them. And the Jewish people will receive Him this time. They will mourn when they see Him because they will recognize that He is the one they have "pierced" (Zechariah 12:10; Revelation 1:7). He will live again in Jerusalem, He will be its glory within and He will be a wall of fire around it. Israel is the holy land. We are witnessing some of the greatest developments in history.

Three Words of Instruction

There are three imperatives here that tell us simply what to do with all of this. The first word is "Come!" In verses 6 and 7 it is the word to the Jewish people, "Come back to the land," because of what God is planning to do there. And they are coming. But it is a word for us too. It is a call to come together, to gather in close to the Lord. His Spirit is with us and He is a wall of fire around us. It is for us to choose to come back from our wandering and to live inside the protection of His provident care.

The second imperative is "shout and be glad" (2:10). Even though our circumstances are discouraging, we need not be discouraged people. There should be something about us that is different because we have seen a vision of the Lord and a vision of the future. With that we can exuberantly celebrate life, we can "shout and be glad." We are energized by this gift of hope, so we can walk triumphantly through discouraging times.

The third word of instruction is "Be still" (2:13). There is a pivotal moment in the book of Revelation, when the seventh seal is broken and the last chapter of history begins to unfold. With that, "there was silence in heaven for about half an hour" (Revelation 8:1). As Jesus steps up to the edge of heaven and prepares to step into the world again, everything in heaven stops with wonder. You can imagine that happening on the night of Jesus' first advent when "the heavens wrapped in wonder, knew the meaning of his birth; in the weakness of a baby they knew God had come to earth."[7] It is going to happen again. Here then, as we sense that the Lord "has roused himself from his holy dwelling" (Zechariah 2:13), it is for us too to stand in wonder at what God is about to do.

I will stand at my watch
  and station myself on the ramparts;
I will look to see what He will say to me. . . .

Lord, I have heard of your fame;
  I stand in awe of your deeds, O Lord.
Renew them in our day,
  in our time make them known;
  in wrath remember mercy. . . .

I heard [all these things] and my heart pounded,
  my lips quivered at the sound;
decay crept into my bones,
  and my legs trembled.
Yet I will wait patiently for the day of calamity
  to come on the nation invading us.
Though the fig tree does not bud
  and there are no grapes on the vines,
though the olive crop fails
  and the fields produce no food,
though there are no sheep in the pen
  and no cattle in the stalls,
yet I will rejoice in the Lord,
  I will be joyful in God my Savior.

The Sovereign Lord is my strength;
  he makes my feet like the feet of a deer,
  he enables me to go on the heights.
(Habakkuk 2:1; 3:2, 16-19)

" 'Shout and be glad, O Daughter of Zion. For I am coming, and I will live among you,' declares the Lord" (Zechariah 2:10). The heart of our hope is the Lord's intention to live among us again.

All of this was very encouraging for the refugee people who had resumed a small scale temple-building project. What they could see was mostly discouraging. They could see the animosity in their Samaritan neighbors. They could see the bleak realities of life in the land—it was hard eking out an existence there. They feared that with a change in emperor everything might become more difficult. Most of them had given up hope that God had remembered them. But what came to them in this powerful vision was not only a picture of God's Angel among them, but an outline of His great plans for them. "Hold on, people! You have little plans that will encourage you a little. God has big plans that should encourage you a lot. He plans to come and live among you again."

There is encouragement here for us too. We are grieved by the immorality that has become so dominant in our land and we wonder when the judgment of God will fall upon us, as surely it must if God is just. We look around at the "New World Disorder" and sense that, even though the Cold War is over, there are many hot wars that have the potential to engulf us. Economic signs are both encouraging and frightening. We are increasingly pressed to recognize that we live in a tense and urgent world. The message is still the same. We need not be discouraged. We need not think that God does not care, that He has withdrawn. We too need to see Him on His red horse standing among the myrtle trees in the valley of God's people. We need to see Him preparing those who are going to cut down the horns of power. We need to see Him laying out His measuring line, planning the place where we are going to live when Jesus comes back to be acknowledged with honor among the Jewish people and all the nations. We must be on edge as we watch this prophecy being fulfilled before our eyes. What a tremendous day to be alive! With the gift of vision, our confidence grows deeper, and we wait in hope.

Discussion Questions for Further Study

1. What projects in your life seem puny and not worth the effort they require? Would it make any difference if you sensed it was part of God's big picture?
2. List some of the big picture things that God is doing in the world.
3. What can you do to be more engaged in what God is doing?
4. What difference would it make if the Lord lived in your home or in your church, and if everything that happened centered around the flame of His presence?
5. In 2:6-7, the call is to come to the Lord. What can you do that will bring you closer to Him?
6. We are also commanded to "shout and be glad." We have seen the Lord, and we have seen the future, so we should have a different perspective. Name two or three specific attitude choices you can make because of that.

Endnotes

[1] Philip Yancey's book, *Disappointment with God* (Grand Rapids, MI: Zondervan Publishing House, 1988), is only one of many that have been presented in recent years, suggesting that many of us struggle with discouragement.

[2] See chapter 1, endnote 1.

[3] Joel 2-3; Amos 5:18-27; 9:1-15; Isaiah 24-27; Zephaniah 1:14-2:3.

[4] The quoting of Deuteronomy 32:10 in Zechariah 2:8 indicates

that this special status will still be in force when this prophecy is fulfilled.

[5] Some interpreters believe that "spiritual Israel" (the Church), and not the literal descendants of Abraham, will receive the benefits of the last day promises. Robert Culver's thesis in his book, *Daniel and the Latter Days* (Chicago: Moody Press, 1954), is that a premillenarian understanding of the book of Daniel is the only approach that can satisfactorily explain it (p. 13). I would make the same argument for the book of Zechariah, though unlike some premillenarians, I will present indicators that suggest that the Church and the people of Israel will share much of the same future (Zechariah 8:20-23, Romans 11:22-24, for example).

[6] Corrie ten Boom, *The Hiding Place* (Minneapolis: Chosen Books, 1971), 86.

[7] Bob Kauflin, "In the First Light," *The Acapella Project* (Nashville: Benson Co., Inc., 1988).

3

A Confident Place to Stand

Zechariah 3:1-10

Then he showed me Joshua the high priest standing before the angel of the LORD, and Satan standing at his right side to accuse him. The LORD said to Satan, "The LORD rebuke you, Satan! The LORD, who has chosen Jerusalem, rebuke you! Is not this man a burning stick snatched from the fire?"

Now Joshua was dressed in filthy clothes as he stood before the angel. The angel said to those who were standing before him, "Take off his filthy clothes."

Then he said to Joshua, "See, I have taken away your sin, and I will put rich garments on you."

Then I said, "Put a clean turban on his head." So they put a clean turban on his head and clothed him, while the angel of the LORD stood by.

The angel of the LORD gave this charge to Joshua: "This is what the LORD Almighty says: 'If you will walk in my ways and keep my requirements, then you will govern my house and have charge of my courts, and I will give you a place among these standing here.

" 'Listen, O high priest Joshua and your associates seated before you, who are men symbolic of things to

come: I am going to bring my servant, the Branch. See, the stone I have set in front of Joshua! There are seven eyes on that one stone, and I will engrave an inscription on it,' says the LORD *Almighty, 'and I will remove the sin of this land in a single day.*

" 'In that day each of you will invite his neighbor to sit under his vine and fig tree,' declares the LORD *Almighty."*

There are occasional moments when we share an exhilarating sense of hope. It happens when we inaugurate a new President, and he boldly proclaims that "the torch has been passed to a new generation of Americans—born in this century"[1] and "this will not be finished in the first one hundred days. Nor will it be finished in the first one thousand days. . . . But let us begin."[2] We sense deeply a shared hope when we participate in the birth of a child, for a few hours choosing to ignore the nastiness of the world awaiting him or her. For just a moment, we simply live in hope, and it is wonderful. All of us in Lexington, Kentucky share a few days of hope at the beginning of a new basketball season when the new team is presented, still undefeated, and we all dare to hope and expect that this year we will hang yet another blue banner from the rafters of Rupp Arena. There is something within us that wants to hope.

So when words of hope come along in the Bible, they reach us viscerally. The book of Zechariah is a message of hope. He too was announcing that a new season of renewal had begun. They weren't inclined to be anything but fearful about their future. Life was hard and their hope had drained away in the sieve of everyday realities. Now comes the word, " 'Return to me,' declares the LORD Almighty, 'and I will return to you' " (1:3). Something new was about to begin. It was a word of hope that was delivered in a forceful form and it resonated deeply.

Haggai was the other preacher at this revival. A month after Zechariah's first message calling for spiritual renewal, the older prophet was the speaker at the public service the day the temple's cornerstone was laid. The message from the Lord was very specific: "From this day on, from this twenty-fourth day of the ninth month, give careful thought to the day when the foundation of the LORD's temple was laid. . . . From this day on I will bless you" (Haggai 2:18-19). They had stepped out in faith and obedience, and the Lord promised His reward for that. He wanted them to live in hope.

Two months later came the vision. It was an exhilarating picture of the Lord in the land, right there among them. C.S. Lewis captures the force of that with his description of Mr. Beaver's confidence in Narnia's winter after receiving word that Aslan was in the land:

> Wrong will be right, when Aslan comes in sight,
> At the sound of his roar, sorrows will be no
> more,
> When he bears his teeth, winter meets its death,
> And when he shakes his mane, we shall have
> spring again.[3]

Hope is renewed with that news. When the vision presents the Lord's dramatic plans, it soon becomes clear that they extend into our lifetime as well. He wants us to live in hope.

In chapters 3 and 4 of Zechariah, there are words of personal encouragement for two men who had good reasons to be low on hope. Joshua and Zerubbabel were still living with the realities of leading an unlikely building project in a city that was a mound of debris. Yet they had stepped out to say, "We can do this and we will! We will believe that God will bless us," and they went to work.

After God discloses what He intends to do for His people before their history is finished, the fourth and the fifth scenes in the vision disclose what He wants to do for His faithful servants who live out their lives in the stress of an unfolding but incomplete process.

We will live spiritually impoverished lives if we do not have a vision of what God wants to do for us. If we construe Christian faith and life to be only doing what God expects, we have discovered only half of His intention—the hard half. We do need to know what He expects of us, but we also need a vision of what He has for us. His intention for us is something deeper.

The Lord had a special provision for Joshua and Zerubbabel, "the two who are anointed to serve the Lord of all the earth" (Zechariah 4:14). Maybe it is important to say that this message is for our leaders first, for these men were Israel's leaders. But all of God's people, His servants, need to sense the specific attention He gives to each one of us. We need a picture of the enriching help He has for those who serve Him, resources and gifts that could be conceived by no one else or provided by no other source. And so these scenes of the vision draw us to Him because we know that we too are stained and powerless.

He Wants to Give You Clean Clothes (3:1-5)

"Then he showed me Joshua the high priest standing before the angel of the LORD, and Satan standing at his right side to accuse him" (3:1).

The venue of the vision has shifted to the court of heaven. What is happening there is very much like the description of the Lord and the accuser contending over Job (Job 1:6-2:7). The temple in Jerusalem was still incomplete, so the high priest was to stand before God, as an intercessor without a formal facility, to represent his people. The Angel of the Lord is that special being who occasionally appears on God's behalf on earth, but here we see his authority in heaven. From heaven's perspective, Joshua was a rather shabby priest, and Satan was standing right there to remind the court (and Joshua) just how shabby he really was.

His argument is not difficult to trace. All of the priests of the Lord are flawed and bear the marks of our sinful race. That is why it was necessary for them to offer a sacrifice for their own sins first (Hebrews 7:26-28). Our enemy can argue that such a man has no right to stand before God, pretending to represent the people of God in holy orders. We feel the force of those accusations too, and we instinctively sense that they are well-grounded. At our best, we know that we really are shabby and sinful. So our confidence before God is eroded by the accusing word.

The importance of the vision is the graphic reassurance that the Lord can look at the same man who is besmirched by the smoke of the world's burning rebellion and offer a different assessment. He rebukes the accuser sharply; He affirms His decision not to abandon His city and this His man; and He removes the filthy clothes that are the marks of his sin and his sinful society. "Then he said to Joshua, 'See, I have taken away your sin, and I will put rich garments on you' " (Zechariah 3:4).

Have you ever wondered what it would be like to be called to stand before God? What would *you* look like if *you* stood in the splendid and pure court of the universe? When Zechariah presented this vision to the people, Joshua would have been sitting in a seat of honor where everyone could see him, surrounded by the other priests and leaders of the people (3:8). It must have been uncomfortable for the high priest to hear, "In God's eyes, you look filthy, Joshua." The accusation of Satan is justified. We *are* filthy. If we recognize anything of our own flaws and failures and sin, we must know that if we were to stand before God, it would be with shame.

But then we see the Lord defending His embarrassed priest and offering an alternate explanation for the filthy clothes. "Is not this man a burning stick snatched from the fire?" (3:2). That at least means, "I brought you all back from the refining fire of Babylon." But because Joshua is singled out here, it is more personal than that. "He is among My chosen. I have been refining him. Even if he bears evidence of having been through the fire, even if the smell and the smoke and the dirt of the experience are still upon him, even if the heat and pressure have exposed his sins, I will take away his sins and put rich garments on him."

The Lord snatches us out of the fire,[4] and then He commands a change of clothes. The promise was so invigorating to Zechariah that he burst out, " 'Put a clean turban on his head [too!].' So they put a clean turban on his head and clothed him, while the angel of the LORD stood by" (3:5). God wanted His people to see that. It is a vision of His intention for us all. How exhilarating!

But that's not all! It is only the beginning. It prepares His man for what's next.

He Wants to Give You a Place (3:6-7)

What follows is a message specifically for Joshua, but the charge and the promise were also for the other leaders. And they are clearly for us as well, because these men are said to be "symbolic of things to come" (3:8).

> This is what the LORD Almighty says: "If you will walk in my ways and keep my requirements, then you will govern my house and have charge of my courts, and *I will give you a place among these standing here*." (3:7, emphasis added)

It is not clear who all was standing there in the presence of the angel of the Lord. We have seen Satan there. Zechariah was a visitor there, with his interpreting angel as a guide. We have seen Joshua standing there, somewhat out of place. We could sketch in the scene, borrowing from the descriptions of heaven given us by other prophetic viewers—all the saints of God, the elders of His people, different creatures otherwise unknown to us, rank upon rank of numberless angelic beings of different sorts and created for different service assignments (Revelation 4-5). At the center of it all is the great Yahweh God Himself, the Creator and Sustainer of it all, dreadful in majesty and holiness and unapproachable light. The experiences of Isaiah and Ezekiel, of Paul and John, when they were caught up into heaven were both inexpressible and overwhelming.[5] Now here is a man who has been reminded of the awfulness of his sin, and the Angel of the Lord is offering him a place to stand.

The Lord had fitted him for that world by taking away his sin and by clothing him in much finer dress than his old ways could ever produce. It was entirely God's gracious choice to so refit this man for service before Him. But now he is charged to wear those clothes carefully, to "walk in my ways and keep my requirements" (Zechariah 3:7). Both his leadership role and his intercessory role would be secured, first by the Lord's choosing and calling, which protected him from the accuser, and then by his own decision to live a holy life. If the diagnosis of his condition was humiliating, if the requirement of holiness ever seemed stiff, the promise of a confident place to stand before God was most uplifting.

Adam and Eve were afraid to stand before God (Genesis 3:8-10). Moses hid his face and was afraid to look (Exodus 3:6). Isaiah had a sense of dread (Isaiah 6:5). Ezekiel was exhausted by the experience (Ezekiel 3:15). Peter was overcome by a sense of his sin (Luke 5:8). Paul was humiliated (Acts 9:8-9). John fell at his feet as though he were dead (Revelation 1:17). David wrote with wonder, "Who may ascend the hill of the LORD? Who may stand in his holy place?" (Psalm 24:3). The invitation to take your place before Him requires some courage. Many choose another way.

Perhaps it is especially important for those who find themselves governing the house of God and having charge of His courts to step up to this. And what a privilege! When Jesus selected twelve to be His disciples, He "designat[ed] them apostles"—they knew from the beginning that they would be sent out to represent Him. Then Mark's account says, He called them to Him, "that they might be with him," and after that, "that he might send them out to preach and to have authority to drive out demons" (Mark 3:13-15).

At the heart of this scene of Zechariah's vision is the Lord calling His priest to stand in His presence, to take his place there, learning to be comfortable living with the realities of the unseen world while continuing to serve in the physical world of brokenness. He was to go back to his responsibilities with new perspective and power.

He Wants to Give You a Promise (3:8-9)

For a refugee people in an unyielding land, this was an uplifting message of hope. Their nation had become a footnote in history, lost among the stories of greater powers. Egypt fell to the Persians, leaving Judah as a minor province in the empire that had overcome all others. But they still dared to hope again—a little. The Lord's answer to that response was this series of pictures to boost their hope yet more. Again He began to show them His larger plans. Their building renewal and their spiritual renewal would be part of a much larger development. There was much more to come!

> "Listen, O high priest Joshua and your associates seated before you, who are men symbolic of things to come: I am going to bring my servant, the Branch. See, the stone I have set in front of Joshua! There are seven eyes on that stone, and I will engrave an inscription on it," says the LORD Almighty, "and I will remove the sin of this land in a single day." (Zechariah 3:8-9)

These brief sentences contain three powerful predictions that stretched Judah's fledgling hope.

The first prediction is the prophecy of the Branch, a messianic figure that would have been understood by Zechariah and the people he addressed, for it had emerged before in their prophetic literature (Isaiah 4:2-6; 11:1-3; Jeremiah 23:5-8; 33:14-18). It was a figure of speech full of hope.

The symbol of the Branch

My wife Joan and I stood in the Garden of Gethsemane one day and heard a tour guide say, "These are the very trees among which Jesus prayed." When I objected that the Romans and the Crusaders cut down everything within miles to build their siege works, and surely the trees in this garden under the shadow of the east wall of the city must have been cut down too, we were told about the olive tree. When you cut it off at the root, it will grow back. It may not be next year, and it may not be for several years. But sooner or later a branch is going to grow out of that stump. It is almost impossible, we were told, to kill an olive tree. Zechariah's vision struck a chord close to the hearts of these people who were familiar with the cultivation of olive trees.

The nation had been cut off. There was no Davidic king and there was little or no national identity. Israel was apparently destroyed. These people were living in the rubble of their homeland and in the rubble of their history. But then, once again, the promise of the Branch came to them. Something was going to grow out of their decapitated roots. They recognized that the Branch would be a supernatural being. No mere human could answer the call of history and step into this role. When the Messiah came, He would be God's man in a special way. His coming and His accomplishments would be a work of God, sketched for their anticipation in the beautiful Hebrew poetry of Isaiah's later messages (Isaiah 60-66). He would emerge, however, from the stump of their national life, a scion of the house of David whose royal throne had been abolished, a continuation of what their Covenant God had done for His people in the past. He would be strong and fruitful, as indestructible as the olive trees that had nourished His people for so many generations. The Lord wanted to remind them of His promise to renew His work among them with this poignant figure.

The symbol of the stone

The second figure of promise is the stone—a symbolic description of the immovable presence of the Lord among them (and among us). He cannot be pushed aside, He cannot be removed and He cannot be ignored. He just sits there in the middle of your life like a rock with eyes all over it. He will watch you—He will watch *over* you.

The seven eyes on the stone indicate that He knows perfectly well; He can see you, no matter where you go. Following Joshua's exposure as a stained and unworthy servant, it may not have been comfortable to be reminded that God's eyes can see everything. But this need not be ominous, because the Lord adds right away, "and I will remove the sin of this land in a single day" (Zechariah 3:9). So all of this colorful language about the filthy garments, about the Branch and about the stone with seven eyes is about removing sin. And that is the third promise.

The removal of sin

There is confidence that comes when your sins are removed, when you are invited to stand before God. Then God begins to show you His intention for the future, further building your confidence. He wants us to live in hope!

Let's Go Back to the Beginning

We really do need to deal with our sin! We stand before the angel of the Lord clothed in soiled garments. All of our rationalizations and self-excusing, our compromises and our petty rebellions, our unkind words, our failures of faith, our inconsistent obedience, our sins large and small, make it easy for the enemy to stand at our elbow and say, "He isn't good enough to be a servant or a priest of Yours." Even our own best-intentioned efforts, our homemade righteousness, is no better than filthy rags (Isaiah 64:6).

Standing before God, we are clothed in shame. Joshua is symbolic of all of us. The removal of his filthy garments and the gift of new, rich clothes and the priest's turban with the gold plate inscribed with "HOLY TO THE LORD" (Exodus 28:36) are symbolic of what Christ the Branch wants to do for us.

He says, "I will remove the sin of this land in a single day" (Zechariah 3:9). We can think of the day that Jesus was on the cross and the words of Isaiah, who said, "the LORD has laid on him the iniquity of us all" (Isaiah 53:6). Or perhaps the single day is a day in your experience when you were overwhelmed by your sinfulness, you came to terms with God's mercy and your need for it, and you bowed before Him in confession. "As far as the east is from the west, so far has he removed our transgressions from us" (Psalm 103:12). We don't have to earn it or keep piling up credit to offset the debit. He just takes it—He removes our sin in a single day. It is a phenomenon that stands with the dramatic prophecy of the Branch and with the figure of the stone as one of the wonders of God.

So His message is, "In all of My planning for the major developments of history, the moving and removing of empires and kings, in all of My planning for that great day when I will return to live among you, I also have a plan for you, Joshua. You don't have to wait for it. You can exchange the filthy clothing of your sin and shabby self-efforts for the rich garments and the turban of honor that I will give you. I am drawing you in closer, taking you deeper. You can take your place here with these. The renewal I have in mind is national, but it is also very personal."

" 'Return to me,' declares the LORD Almighty, 'and I will return to you' " (1:3). It is a message of hope.

And a Footnote . . . (3:10)

In the last line of the chapter, the richness of this blessing is stated in language the people of Judah would have understood well: "In that day each of you will invite his neighbor to sit under his vine and fig tree" (3:10). The vine and the fig tree are the symbols of God's gracious giving. In this chapter it begins with the gift of clean clothes, it extends through the gift of a place to stand before God and the gift of a strong hope. Then it ends with the gift of nourishment and rest.

In contrast to Jonah who sat miserably in the shade of the vine God had given him, angry about God's gift of mercy (Jonah 4), here is the picture of a grateful heart, eager to share his mercy with his neighbor—much like the sinful woman who loved Jesus so much because she had been forgiven so much. Here is the filthy made clean, walking in confidence before the Lord Almighty and knowing how privileged he is to live in this shade. Inviting his neighbor to join him there is the natural conclusion of this life-changing sequence. It is "friendship evangelism" not prompted by the pressure of the preacher, but a natural extension of the awe we feel for the great work of God in removing our sin.

Joshua's deep cleansing, place of privilege and newfound hope would drastically change his life in three short strokes! He was instructed not to keep these blessings for himself!

Dear Lord, do it for us too, and we will extend the shade of our vine and fig tree to our neighbors as well!

Discussion Questions for Further Study

1. What circumstances or thought patterns drain away your natural reserve of hope?
2. What can Satan rightly accuse you of before God? Where are you especially vulnerable to the accuser?
3. Picture God giving you something else for each of your dirty garments. What would you like Him to give you to replace what is stained?
4. The Lord said to Joshua, "If you will walk in my ways and keep my requirements . . ." (3:7). Which of the Lord's "ways" and "requirements" should you be more careful to observe?
5. Imagine you are invited to take your place before God. Seeing your life from that perspective, what would look different to you?
6. What are the three promises of God in Zechariah 3 that are meant to make you hopeful about the future?
7. Are you ever uncomfortable being reminded that the Lord's eye is upon you? Perhaps it would be profitable for you to find someone with whom you can share your feelings.
8. Now it's confession time. From your consideration of this chapter in Zechariah, what has the Lord touched in your life that needs to be taken care of? Be firm about it—make a list!
9. Consider who in your circle of family, friends and acquaintances needs to be invited to sit under the tree of God's blessing. It's time to share your shade!

Endnotes

[1] John F. Kennedy, "Inaugural Address," *The American Reader:*

Words That Moved a Nation, Diane Ravitch, ed. (New York: Harper Collins Publishers, 1990), 315.

[2] Ibid., 316.

[3] C.S. Lewis, *The Lion, the Witch, and the Wardrobe* (New York: Harper Trophy, 1950), 79.

[4] It seems that Jude sensed the dramatic nature of this saving work of God when he exhorted his readers to "snatch others from the fire and save them" too (Jude 23).

[5] Isaiah 6:1-8; Ezekiel 1:1-3:15; 2 Corinthians 12:1-6; Revelation 1:1-18.

4

A Steady Supply of Oil

Zechariah 4:1-14

Then the angel who talked with me returned and wakened me, as a man is wakened from his sleep. He asked me, "What do you see?"

I answered, "I see a solid gold lampstand with a bowl at the top and seven lights on it, with seven channels to the lights. Also there are two olive trees by it, one on the right of the bowl and the other on its left."

I asked the angel who talked with me, "What are these, my lord?"

He answered, "Do you not know what these are?"

"No, my lord," I replied.

So he said to me, "This is the word of the Lord *to Zerubbabel: 'Not by might nor by power, but by my Spirit,' says the* Lord *Almighty.*

"What are you, O mighty mountain? Before Zerubbabel you will become level ground. Then he will bring out the capstone to shouts of 'God bless it! God bless it!' "

Then the word of the Lord *came to me: "The hands of Zerubbabel have laid the foundation of this temple;*

his hands will also complete it. Then you will know that the Lord *Almighty has sent me to you.*

"Who despises the day of small things? Men will rejoice when they see the plumb line in the hand of Zerubbabel.

"(These seven are the eyes of the Lord, *which range throughout the earth.)"*

Then I asked the angel, "What are these two olive trees on the right and the left of the lampstand?"

Again I asked him, "What are these two olive branches beside the two gold pipes that pour out golden oil?"

He replied, "Do you not know what these are?"

"No, my lord," I said.

So he said, "These are the two who are anointed to serve the Lord of all the earth."

What Zechariah sees next is a message for another of God's servant leaders. After a brief rest (we can only imagine how exhausting it must be to tour through the realities of the world on the other side), the next scene of the vision unfolds.

"Not by Might nor by Power" (4:1-10)

The lampstand that Zechariah described was not unfamiliar to the Jewish people, though most of them had never seen it. It was the menorah—the ornate seven-branched lampstand in the holy place of the temple where only the priests were permitted to enter. There had been one in the Tabernacle (Exodus 25:31-40) and ten in Solomon's temple (2 Chronicles 4:7). There would again be one in the new temple that was under construction. A picture of that menorah was chiseled into the Arch of Titus on the Sacred Way near the Forum in Rome to celebrate Titus' ravaging of the Jews. It portrays him carrying off their sacred vessels and other things as a symbol of his conquest.[1]

The menorah was not a symbol of conquest but of prayer. The lamps were trimmed and refueled continually. Their incessant burning in the temple represented continual prayer. In some Christian traditions, candles are used in the same way to help worshipers visualize their prayers always ascending before the Lord. What Zechariah saw in this fifth scene of his vision was describing something important and familiar.

But there was an innovation in the design. There was a bowl on top, with channels coming down from the bowl to the lamps. Zechariah wasn't sure what this was all about.

> "Do you not know what these are?"
>
> "No, my lord," I replied.
>
> So he said to me: "This is the word of the LORD to Zerubbabel: 'Not by might nor by power, but by my Spirit,' says the LORD Almighty." (4:4-6)

This time the word of hope and encouragement was for Zerubbabel.

Zerubbabel was a special figure in Judah's story. He was the grandson of Jehoiachin, the king of Judah taken captive by Nebuchadnezzar in the second deportation to Babylon. Jehoiachin was imprisoned for thirty-seven years and then, with a change in imperial policy, he was restored to a place of high honor as a vassal king at the table of the short-lived successor of

Nebuchadnezzar named Evil-Merodach. Jehoiachin was the last legitimate heir of David to sit on the throne, though Zedekiah (his uncle) followed him (2 Kings 24:8-20; 25:27-30).

Zerubbabel was his grandson. If there were still a throne, and if there were still a nation, he would have been a king. He was recognized by the Jews as a prince of the house of David, and he was appointed by the Persians to be their governor. Yet he was granted very little authority. He may have been their leader, but he had to exercise his leadership under the heavy hand of the empire and under the jealous and powerful scrutiny of the governor of Trans-Euphrates.

The circumstances were genuinely barren of hope. Yet with the preaching of Haggai and Zechariah and the vision of what God was doing and planning, expectations of dramatic developments for a strong future were emerging again.

Ironically, all of that put Zerubbabel in an awkward position. Like many who have come into leadership without seeking it, he was fearful he would now be expected to lead Judah to an impossible dream not of his making. He was the leader of a struggling refugee people, standing in the ruins of an ancient nation and a magnificent city, now saddled with an unrealistic vision. He didn't have a fraction of the might or the political power that it would take to make the vision a reality. *Who am I to dream of throwing down the horns of the nations that have oppressed my people?* he may have wondered. *Who am I to dream of leading these people into prosperity, a renewal of our national life and the rebuilding of the capital city?*

The vision of the solid gold lampstand was a personal message for Zerubbabel. The old lampstand supported seven oil lamps which were kept aflame by the careful, faithful work of the priests who trimmed the wicks and filled the lamps with oil. Faithful service was at the heart of the old order. But Zerubbabel could look back over the sixteen years since he had taken leadership of this nation-rebuilding venture and he could see that his faithful work had accomplished nothing remarkable. The grand dreams of the future that came with Zechariah's vision were clearly beyond the range of his abilities. He seemed more suited to maintenance tasks than to bold new ventures.

But the innovation in the envisioned menorah held the key for Zerubbabel. The reservoir at the top, ingeniously connected to each lamp by a new channel, would constantly fill each with oil. The lamp of the nation's life would be fueled by a new, uninterrupted flow. The life of the nation's leader would be energized by this new source. The vision now opening up before them all would come to life not because of the faithful service of the old order but because of the work of the Spirit of God continually bringing the resources and the power of the Lord Almighty to their circumstances and their national life. "This is the word of the Lord to Zerubbabel: 'These great new developments that God is planning for you will not be accomplished by human might nor by political power but by my Spirit flowing into your life,' says the Lord Almighty. 'I will give you a steady supply.' "

Then Zerubbabel is further encouraged with some specific predictions: 1) The impossible will become easy, the mountain will become level ground before him; 2) Having just laid the cornerstone of the new temple, he will also be the one to set in place the capstone with great rejoicing; 3) With this development, it will become clear to all that Zerubbabel is God's man, not just because of his lineage, but because of God's special choosing; 4) When he steps forward more assertively to lead them in this project, the people will respond with joy, including even those who have grumbled that what they were doing was insignificant and small.

This "be strong and courageous" message concludes with another reminder that the stone with seven eyes, "the eyes of the LORD, which range throughout the earth" (Zechariah 4:10) is an ever-present rock of strength among them, rising up from the floor of their desert like Ayers Rock in Australia's Northern Territory. For Joshua, the stone had symbolized the Lord's intention to be right there to watch him and to keep him pure and fit for His holy service. For Zerubbabel, the stone symbolized the Lord's intention to stand strong among His people, to keep His eye on their building project and all of their service for Him, and to make sure that what He intended for them would come to pass.

"Anointed to Serve the Lord of All the Earth" (4:11-14)

"Then I asked the angel, 'What are these two olive trees on the right and the left of the lampstand?' . . . So he said, 'These are the two who are anointed to serve the Lord of all the earth' " (4:11, 14).

Joshua needed to see a picture of how shabby he looked before the Lord and what the Lord wanted to do *for* him. Zerubbabel needed to see how large the Lord's plans were and what He wanted to do *through* him.

The vision communicated to Joshua and Zerubbabel that they were, as the olive trees on the right and the left of the lampstand, the two "anointed to serve the Lord of all the earth" as the priest of His people and as their leader. They were to see the work of the Spirit in the middle of the picture, the lampstand with the constant flow of oil. And they were to view themselves as strong and perennial as olive trees. Their work would stand with the work of the Spirit. Joshua's keeping God's courts and standing before Him was a small precursor of a much greater work of governance and atonement yet to come. Zerubbabel's placing of the last stone of the temple would lead people to praise the Lord with jubilant shouting and realize that facing the impossible with God is a simple delight.

The rock that was the heavy weight with penetrating eyes, exposing their sin, became the presence of the Lord looking upon them with favor wherever they would go throughout the whole earth.

Conclusion

These two chapters are special messages for two of the Lord Almighty's servants. We must also see the encouragement here for us, encouragement that He knows each one of us and what we need. Even though our natural perspective limits us to a sinking sense of our sinfulness and a survey of the mountains that will not move, He knows how to show us what He can do for us and what He can do through us. The message is for us too. He is reorienting us and drawing us into a deeper spirituality.

We may sense some shame, as Joshua surely must have, to recognize how sin stains our lives. It adheres to us like dirt on our shoes. Some of that is because of where we walk. But we must humbly acknowledge that it also rises from the perversity in our natures. We are embarrassed to recognize how often we try to do what we do, even our work for God, in our own might and power. We can take more of the credit if we do it ourselves, of course. But in the light of this vision, that perversity is sin.

In the early part of this century, this twin message was raised in England by a man named Rodney "Gypsy" Smith. He was born in a gypsy's covered wagon in East Anglia, and he lived there for the early years of his life. He grew to be a brilliant man, educated at Cambridge. More than that, it was clear that God's hand was upon him. Thousands responded to his simple presentations of the gospel. Revival followed him wherever he went.[2]

Someone asked Gypsy Smith one day how to have a revival. His answer was profoundly penetrating. "Do you have a place where you can pray?"

The man said, "Yes, I do."

Smith said, "Get a piece of chalk, go to your place of prayer, get down on your knees, and draw a circle around yourself. Then pray to God to send revival on everything inside the circle, and stay there until He answers. If you do, you will have revival."[3]

We wait for it to begin somewhere else. We think that it must not be for our generation that the Lord has abandoned us, that the best work of God is now happening overseas, that it was an eighteenth- and nineteenth-century phenomenon of special events mysteriously emerging out of the sovereign will of an inscrutable God—not to be expected or impudently sought by religious experience junkies. But the word of the Lord through this prophet was, "Return to me," says the Lord, "and I will return to you. Let me show you what I am thinking and feeling and planning." And then He adds these personal messages: "The promise is for you, Joshua; it is for you, Zerubbabel. First of all, let Me give you some clean clothes. Second, let Me give you a supply that will never stop. If you come back to Me, I will surely come back to you with all of this."

In all of the dramatic, history-shaping work the Lord is doing in Israel, Russia and so many corners of the world, He is also intervening in the lives of each of us, His servants. The vision is a picture for us too. He is here to protect us from the accusing enemy, to take away our sin, to give us new rich garments, to give us His Spirit and to give success to our work. At the end of the scene, we are as solid and fruitful as olive trees, we are those "anointed to serve the Lord of all the earth" (4:14) and we are called up to a higher standard of holiness and faith-filled leadership.

Discussion Questions for Further Study

1. What dreams and expectations do you have that sometimes seem to be impossible mountains?
2. Read slowly through John 15:1-17. How can you more effectively keep your connection with Christ secured so that His life will flow into yours? What difference will that make?

3. What is the Lord doing in your life and work for which He should be given the credit?
4. Are your ambitions generally small enough for you to accomplish without the Lord's help? How might He want to expand your vision?
5. Is there a task before you that you should assertively step into?
6. In what ways are you to be like one of the olive trees in the vision?

Endnotes

[1] Abraham Negev, ed. "Menorah," *The Archaeological Encyclopedia of the Holy Land*, rev. ed. (Nashville, TN: Thomas Nelson Publishers, 1986), 239-40.

[2] J.D. Douglas, ed., "Smith, Rodney ("Gypsy"), *The New International Dictionary of the Christian Church* (Grand Rapids. MI: Zondervan Publishing House, 1974), 910.

[3] Paul Lee Tan, "How to Start a Revival," *Encyclopedia of 7,700 Illustrations: Signs of the Times* (Rockville, MD: Assurance Publishers, 1979), 1152.

5

Ten Ways to Forfeit the Blessings of God

Zechariah 5:1-11

I looked again—and there before me was a flying scroll!

He asked me, "What do you see?"

I answered, "I see a flying scroll, thirty feet long and fifteen feet wide."

And he said to me, "This is the curse that is going out over the whole land; for according to what it says on one side, every thief will be banished, and according to what it says on the other, everyone who swears falsely will be banished. The Lord *Almighty declares, 'I will send it out, and it will enter the house of the thief and the house of him who swears falsely by my name. It will remain in his house and destroy it, both its timbers and its stones.' "*

Then the angel who was speaking to me came forward and said to me, "Look up and see what this is that is appearing."

I asked, "What is it?"

He replied, "It is a measuring basket." And he added, "This is the iniquity of the people throughout the land."

Then the cover of lead was raised, and there in the basket sat a woman! He said, "This is wickedness," and he pushed her back into the basket and pushed the lead cover down over its mouth.

Then I looked up—and there before me were two women, with the wind in their wings! They had wings like those of a stork, and they lifted up the basket between heaven and earth.

"Where are they taking the basket?" I asked the angel who was speaking to me.

He replied, "To the country of Babylonia to build a house for it. When it is ready, the basket will be set there in its place."

The first five scenes of the vision were all very encouraging to the people of Judah, each one promising that the Lord would intervene and that He would introduce blessing again into the landscape of their bleak lives. God was encouraging a new commitment to return to Him by helping them visualize His promise to return to them, giving them a sense of what that would be. He was nurturing both their hope and their desire.

Zechariah saw the Lord with them in their valley, feeling the distress they felt and planning better things for them. He saw the powerful forces opposing them and their remarkable destruction. He saw the Lord's preparations to come back to a renewed city. He saw the high priest given a place to stand in the Lord's presence and their leader given a steady flow of the Spirit of God to fuel his work. All of this was a look into another reality, every bit as real as the one with which we are familiar.

The tone changes in scenes six and seven. They are a warning that not all of Judah's people would receive those blessings. If we were to follow the Zechariah story, we would discover his generation finished the temple—but that was about all the blessing they enjoyed.

The promises of God were clear. He showed them that He was already working on the good things that were to come to them. But in this chapter, what becomes just as clear was that not everyone who was working on the temple would inherit those good things. In fact, what some would inherit would be very much like the horrible judgment that fell on their grandparents' generation. What we are shown here is a hard reality. But it is one that we need to see.

We may not know at first what to make of the scroll, the basket with the woman in it and the women with wings like a stork. It is all about sin. It seems there was a widespread disregard for the law of God in the land (5:6). In future generations, a concern for the law of God would become central to their religious experience, a backlash to the moral laxity of previous generations that became stifling and legalistic.[1] But at this point folks apparently thought they could work on the temple which they had started to rebuild and continue to live in sin, all the while expecting God to bless them. They didn't seem to sense the absurdity of trying to walk on both sides of that street at the same time. Sin can be so common that it becomes normal.[2] They came to accept it in their land and in themselves and they learned to work around it; and they came to expect God to accept it and work around it as well.

The next two scenes of the vision intruded with another perspective. The people needed to see this too—to see sin for the plague and the threat that it really is. The theme here picks up the promise in Zechariah 3:9 where the Angel of the Lord said to Joshua, who had just been given new clean rich garments, "I will remove the sin of this land in a single day." They needed to see God's plans for dealing with sin—two initiatives He had in mind to deal with the problem of evil. And they needed to be warned that if their sin wasn't taken care of they would forfeit the blessing. Let's look at these kaleidoscopic images more closely.

Scene Six: The Flying Scroll (5:1-4)

The flying scroll tells of a curse over the whole land. The scroll was not rolled up in a case and stacked neatly in the place of honor in the temple or the synagogue, as you would expect of a sacred scroll. But it was open and flying, flapping in the wind like a flag. It was very large and it was there for all to see. Everybody knew what the scroll said.

The scroll was a copy of the Ten Commandments. And the concern was specifically about the eighth commandment and the third commandment—stealing and using the Lord's name in an insincere oath. Perhaps these were common abuses at the time—and they still are. We diddle with the truth, we fudge on our taxes, we keep things that we do not own. Our transgressions are not so blatant that they haunt our consciences, and as conscience erodes there is room for more fudge. In desperate circumstances we allow ourselves to get involved in theft and perjury (finding softer words to avoid the force of these commandments, of course). And still we expect God to bless us for our contribution to the temple project.

Beyond that, it is likely that two commandments, one on each side of the scroll, stand merely as examples of "the iniquity of the people throughout the land" (5:6). The figure of speech used here is synecdoche, where a part stands for the whole.[3] It is not much of a stretch to suggest that violation of these two commandments was a pointed way of condemning Judah's spiritual carelessness toward the whole law. Their moral compass had become defective. They no longer saw spiritual realities clearly. They needed to be shown the commandments flapping over them like a curse.

What Zechariah saw on one side of that banner flapping in the breeze was the second table of the Law, where we learn that everyone who wrongs his or her neighbor violates the final six commandments of the law of God. On the other side was the first table of the Law, the first four commandments, which taught God's people to carefully regard His holiness. That flying scroll posted ten ways that they could forfeit the blessing of God. Built into the covenant of the law was the principle that those who kept the commandments would prosper and those who did not would meet with disaster. The previous scenes of the vision promised God's intervention and blessing if they returned to Him. Now the other side of the covenant is brought to them in living color—the promise of a curse if they did not.

The vision goes on to remind them what Jewish law prescribed for the homes of people who had infectious diseases like leprosy. It was so fearful that there was a detailed body of legislation in Leviticus to teach them how to deal with it, including in the worst scenario the destruction of the lepers' homes so that the plague would be arrested right there (Leviticus 14:32-45). The infection of sin, the vision warned, would be treated in like manner!

One of the apparently most God-careless people of modern times was Charles Darwin, who gave us *On the Origin of Species* and other bedevilment. He ignored God and tried to describe the world as if God were not there. That has set a standard for all of our modern age—you can make sense of everything without any reference to God. It is clear however, on a closer reading of his life, that Darwin formulated his theories of origins in a "pervasive anxiety" about where his thinking was taking him—into conflict with the church of his heritage and his godly wife. And he was aware that materialism launched the horrors of the French Revolution.[4] He could not get away from it. God flies His banner in the sky over us all, no matter how hard we try to avoid it. Nobody can plead ignorance, for the scroll is large enough for all to see and none can escape its judgment.

In the fourth century B.C., the city of Syracuse, a Greek colony on the island of Sicily, was ruled by a tyrant named Dionysius the Elder. Picture an elaborate court around him where he dispensed favor and power. The Roman orator Cicero told a story of a man in his court named Damocles. This courtier sought advantage by flattering the cruel tyrant. He was both obsequious and obnoxious. One day after an especially elaborate flourish of praise, the story goes,

Dionysius stood to his feet, clapped his hands and said, "Declare that tomorrow night there shall be a banquet in the honor of my great friend Damocles."

The next twenty-four hours were very heady for the man of honor, and he was escorted with great pride into the Grand Hall, carried to his seat of prominence by stirring music. When all were seated the mood was strangely serious. He looked around and sensed that many people were staring at him. It was also clear that the others were staring at something that was above him. When he dared to carefully look up, Damocles saw to his horror an enormous sword suspended over him, hanging by a single hair. "So Dionysius expressed his contempt for the flatterer," and so "the Sword of Damocles" comes into our language as a figure of speech for deadly peril, but only sometimes perceived.[5]

The scroll of the commandments was the curse that hung above the land of Judah. Such a bold, clear pronouncement of punishment for sin should have spurred these people on to repentance and righteousness. Sadly, there is no evidence that it did. They apparently proceeded as they were. God gave them their temple building, but it was seventy-five years before Ezra and Nehemiah came to Jerusalem and the blessing began to flow. It skipped an entire generation because they did not deal with sin as they should have.

Scene Seven: The Measuring (5:5-11)

God has another plan for dealing with sin, portrayed in the seventh scene of the vision—the one about the measuring basket and the removal of wickedness.

> Then the angel who was speaking to me came forward and said to me, "Look up and see what this is that is appearing."
> I asked, "What is it?"
> He replied, "It is a measuring basket [an ephah]." And he added, "This is the iniquity of the people throughout the land." (5:5-6)

The ephah, a basket slightly larger than a bushel, was already a symbol of sin for the Jewish people. It was common for them to be cheated by a merchant who had a dishonest measure—passing off the contents of a smaller basket as an ephah of corn or an ephah of flour. Micah preached a very angry sermon against people who did that (Micah 6:9-16).

In Zechariah's vision, the ephah symbolizes pervasive injustice, "the iniquity of the people throughout the land." Perhaps you could say that wickedness was there by the bushelful. "Throughout the land" suggests that this now is about more than personal sin. Sometimes a pattern of sin is endemic—it is just everywhere. You get drawn into it, you cannot seem to move it, you learn to accommodate to it. You try to ignore it but it is there. It can be like the demon that retorted to the elders of our church who were insisting on its removal, "I have been in this family for ten generations, and I'm not leaving just because you tell me to." Sometimes evil is well-rooted.

The life of the community was contaminated by sin that had become common. Haggai said, " 'So it is with this people and this nation in my sight,' declares the LORD. 'Whatever they do and whatever they offer [in worship] is defiled' " (Haggai 2:14). The dishonesty that prompted the making of false measures was a symptom of an underlying perversity that infected all of life. This scene of the vision was about the need of their land to be cleansed of sin. It is a pressing concern for some of us too.

Their neighbors would later be called "Samaritans." They had been imported by the Assyrian Shalmaneser a few generations back after he had destroyed the northern nation and taken most of the Israelites elsewhere. According to their ancient custom they brought some of their ancestral gods with them, but they also wanted to worship the gods of the land that was their new home. So their religion was a mishmash, whatever blend seemed good to them. It was also in some ways less demanding than the puritanical scruples these prophets were preaching (2 Kings 17:24-41). That kind of mix-and-match approach to life had a certain allure to it, and it was endemic in Judea, the angel said—in fact it was as common as a crooked set of scales.

"Then the cover of lead was raised, and there in the basket sat a woman! He said, 'This is wickedness,' and he pushed her back into the basket and pushed the lead cover down over its mouth" (Zechariah 5:7-8). It is not important that the figure of wickedness is female. Evil is portrayed in both genders in the Bible. But what we need to see here is that evil has a face. There is a real Evil One, and as we see in this picture she is mostly hidden from sight. But she is struggling to break out, she is attempting to escape and run freely through the land. The angel with superior strength is able to confine her, though clearly there is a struggle. There is a corresponding description of this tension in Second Thessalonians 2, about the "man of lawlessness," who

> will oppose and will exalt himself over everything that is called God or is worshiped. . . . And now you know what is holding him back, so that he may be revealed at the proper time. For the secret power of lawlessness is already at work; but the one who now holds it back will continue to do so till he is taken out of the way. And then the lawless one will be revealed, whom the Lord Jesus will overthrow with the breath of his mouth and destroy by the splendor of his coming. (2 Thessalonians 2:4, 6-8)

What follows is a great picture of what the Lord does with sin. First He keeps the lid on it! And in the end He will remove the whole basket.

"Then I looked up—and there before me were two women, with the wind in their wings! They had wings like those of a stork, and they lifted up the basket between heaven and earth" (Zechariah 5:9). This is a classic picture of angels who are portrayed elsewhere in Scripture in other forms.[6] These two are assigned a special task, part of the Lord's plan for dealing with sin. We saw the Lord step in to remove Joshua's filthy garments. We heard Him say that He would destroy the houses of those who ignore the curse that flies over them. Here now is the picture of a future day when He will step in and take away the pervasive evil in the land altogether.

In Zechariah 2:12 the land is called the "holy land." The Lord wanted to say in reassuring language that

He would choose to give favor to the land again, and He would come to live among them there. Our use of the term is much more casual, though the Israeli Government Tourist Office tries to generate some special aura around it. "Jesus walked here and so should you. Come and spend money." And 6 million people do every year! My wife and I find it disorienting to sense just how secular Israel really is. There certainly is religion there, but not much spirituality. In fact, that land will not really be holy until the angels take the sin to Babylon.

But God promised to make that happen! The wind of the spirit in the wings of the angels is the Spirit of God. It is a word of God—He intends to look after that pervasive evil.

The rest of what He says is very sobering. It is a hint of things to come—of a final battle with evil at the end of time, described more fully in later chapters in this prophetic book. But this is a unique contribution to that composite picture. A house, perhaps a house of worship, will be built where incarnate evil will reign supreme. When it is ready, the basket will be put in its place. Babylon was the seat of godless power to them. The first organized revolt against God occurred in Babylon, and that is when God confounded our languages to prevent total opposition to Him (Genesis 11:1-9). The evil regime that took Judah captive was from Babylon. In John's Revelation, Babylon is again the center of opposition to God (Revelation 18). Whether that is figurative or real can be argued, but the fact is that sin will not only find a home there, but a house will be prepared where it can be set up on a pedestal to be honored by people who are opposed to God. At the end of time, God will remove the measuring basket full of evil from the holy land, a great polarization between good and evil will emerge out of the murky morality of our world of grays, and a tremendous battle will take place.

God Will Triumph!

We are meant to see here God's ability to pack up evil and literally ship it to the center of wickedness where He will deal with it. The living power of evil must be banished from the land. God's power will keep the lid on evil's toxic influence and someday will take it all away. The only successful way to deal with evil conclusively is to remove it completely. One way or another, God will do that.

The word in chapter 3 that God would remove the sin of the land in a single day was a word of encouragement. Here the same message is much more harsh. In fact, harsh is the only way to deal with sin, and harsh is what God will be if we do not take His offer of clean clothes in scene four. The lesson here is a warning that pervasive sin in our lives and in our land is enough to cancel the blessing that should come to us when we are working on His Church. The message now is that when God hands out the blessings that have richly filled the first five scenes of this vision, He may skip a generation and He may skip you if you have not dealt with your sin.

So living carefully by God's moral standards is not just an optional extra for those who want to be supercharged spiritually, as if you are free to make up the pattern of life as you wish. Somebody needs to stand up in the middle of a sermon series about the renewed blessings of God and say, "You don't get the blessing if you don't follow the commandments! God is waving a banner before you. Pay attention. The thief will be banished, everyone who swears falsely will be banished—banished from the covenant, banished from the blessing. You step outside of the circle of promised blessing when you choose to live in sin."

"The LORD Almighty declares, 'I will send it out [the curse], and it will enter the house of the thief and the house of him who swears falsely by my name. It will remain in his house and destroy it, both its timbers and its stones' " (Zechariah 5:4). No one who persists in disobedience will go unpunished. God's Word will go right to the private places where the police force of your land cannot find you, to the privacy of your home and your thoughts. He will purge the land of chronic covenant breakers. Both the thief and the perjurer can expect to be expelled.

The scroll reminds us that everybody knows this. It is an enormous reality over us all, an instinct for right and wrong that is towed like a banner behind an airplane through our consciences. It is clear to everyone, no matter how hard we try to pretend that it is not there so we can avoid its implications. It was visualized for the prophet in dramatic form as an imposing copy of the commandments flapping in the wind.

Just when you thought you were getting ahead with your own homemade blend of good work and compromise—building on the temple while freely fiddling with the truth, contributing financially to the project while cheating in your business, serving the Lord while nurturing your own pride, serving the

Lord and serving yourself, just when you think that the Lord, in His promise of blessing and forgiveness revealed so dramatically to the prophet, overrides your sin because He is so gracious and merciful, the vision comes around to a picture of the destruction that is suspended over you, ready to enter your house and destroy it, both timbers and stones. God's plan for dealing with sin is to destroy those who insist on living in it.

One way or another, God will deal with sin. In fact He is already removing sin as we yield to Him. And He promises:

> For as high as the heavens are above the earth,
> so great is his love for those who fear him;
> as far as the east is from the west,
> so far has he removed our transgressions from us.
> (Psalm 103:11-12)

And concerning the impulse of sin that we feel inside, God says:

> I will give them singleness of heart and action, so that they will always fear me for their own good and the good of their children after them. I will make an everlasting covenant with them: I will never stop doing good to them, and I will inspire them to fear me, so that they will never turn away from me. (Jeremiah 32:39-40)

God can do that! Ezekiel was a priest using the language of ritual washing when he said,

> I will sprinkle clean water on you, and you will be clean; I will cleanse you from all your impurities and from all your idols. I will give you a new heart and put a new spirit in you; I will remove from you your heart of stone and give you a heart of flesh. And I will put my Spirit in you and move you to follow my decrees and be careful to keep my laws. You will live in the land I gave your forefathers; you will be my people, and I will be your God. I will save you from all your uncleanness. (Ezekiel 36:25-29)

> Joshua was dressed in filthy clothes as he stood before the angel . . . [who] said to those who were standing before him, "Take off his filthy clothes."
>
> Then he said to Joshua, "See, I have taken away your sin, and I will put rich garments on you." (Zechariah 3:3-4)

And so God "justifies the sinner" as we say. He has two plans for dealing with the plague of sin. He will destroy those who insist on living in it and He will remove it completely.

> "Since we have these promises, dear friends, let us purify ourselves from everything that contaminates body and spirit, perfecting holiness out of reverence for God." (2 Corinthians 7:1)

"Father, I want to know Thee, but my cowardly heart fears to give up its toys. I cannot part with them without inward bleeding, and I do not try to hide from Thee the

terror of the parting. I come trembling, but I do come. Please root from my heart all those things which I have cherished so long and which have become a very part of my living self, so that Thou mayest enter and dwell there without a rival. Then shalt Thou make the place of Thy feet glorious. Then shall my heart have no need of the sun to shine in it, for Thyself wilt be the light of it, and there shall be no night there."[7]

Discussion Questions for Further Study

1. What is so corrosive about sin that it can be compared to leprosy? Identify some of the damage it causes.
2. If the picture of the woman in the basket is a depiction of the Evil One straining to be released into the world, what are some of the details here that help us understand sin in the world and how God handles it?
3. Consider your inner struggle with sin. Identify those aspects of your life that the Lord is seeking to clean up.
4. Work your way slowly through Psalm 103:11-12; Jeremiah 32:39-40; Ezekiel 36:25-29; Zechariah 3:3-4; 2 Corinthians 7:1. Ask the Lord to do His cleansing work in your life.

Endnotes

[1] Ezra "devoted himself to the study and observance of the Law of the LORD, and to teaching its decrees and laws in Israel" (Ezra 7:10). With that, the foundations for a national revival were laid. The Pharisees of Jesus' time traced their roots back to Ezra, but they were a tragic shadow of what had been a mighty movement.

[2] Not many years later, Malachi's scorching sermons expose

the same duplicity: insincere temple service, insincere marriage vows, withholding the tithe . . . "You have not set your heart to honor me" (Malachi 2:2).

3 For example, we say that Bluebeard's men were "cutthroats," meaning they were absolutely ruthless. Some of them actually did cut people's throats, we may be sure, and we allow the description of the few to shape the reputation of them all. Or we know what is meant when a farmer says he has five hired hands. Of course he means that he has five hired helpers, and usually that means he really has ten hired hands. A part stands for the whole. Violation of those two commandments, which may have been especially pervasive at the time, was a pointed way of condemning their carelessness for the whole law.

4 John Bowlby, *Charles Darwin: A New Life* (New York: W.W. Norton & Company, 1991), 212-213.

5 Paul Lee Tan, "Sword of Damocles," *Encyclopedia of 7,700 Illustrations: Signs of the Times* (Rockville, MD: Assurance Publishers, 1979), 451; and Donald W. Bradeen, "Damocles," *The World Book Encyclopedia*, 1980, vol. v, 16.

6 The seraphim that Isaiah saw had six wings. Sometimes angels appear to be humanoid in form. There are also creatures in heaven that are unlike any of the species in our world. They may have worship tasks or messenger tasks, some are clearly assigned to assist God's people on earth and many are the Lord's warrior hosts to fight the great battles of the War of the Worlds. But this is our favorite picture of angels—creatures so beautiful that they must be women, with wings like a stork, doing His work.

7 A.W. Tozer, *The Pursuit of God* (Camp Hill, PA: Christian Publications, 1982), 30-31.

6

Setting the Stage for the Lord's Return

Zechariah 6:1-15

I looked up again—and there before me were four chariots coming out from between two mountains—mountains of bronze! The first chariot had red horses, the second black, the third white, and the fourth dappled—all of them powerful. I asked the angel who was speaking to me, "What are these, my lord?"

The angel answered me, "These are the four spirits of heaven, going out from standing in the presence of the Lord of the whole world. The one with the black horses is going toward the north country, the one with the white horses toward the west, and the one with the dappled horses toward the south."

When the powerful horses went out, they were straining to go throughout the earth. And he said, "Go throughout the earth!" So they went throughout the earth.

Then he called to me, "Look, those going toward the north country have given my Spirit rest in the land of the north."

The word of the Lord *came to me: "Take silver and*

gold from the exiles Heldai, Tobijah and Jedaiah, who have arrived from Babylon. Go the same day to the house of Josiah son of Zephaniah. Take the silver and gold and make a crown, and set it on the head of the high priest, Joshua son of Jehozadak. Tell him this is what the Lord *Almighty says: 'Here is the man whose name is the Branch, and he will branch out from his place and build the temple of the* Lord*. It is he who will build the temple of the* Lord*, and he will be clothed with majesty and will sit and rule on his throne. And he will be a priest on his throne. And there will be harmony between the two.' The crown will be given to Heldai, Tobijah, Jedaiah and Hen son of Zephaniah as a memorial in the temple of the* Lord*. Those who are far away will come and help to build the temple of the* Lord*, and you will know that the* Lord *Almighty has sent me to you. This will happen if you diligently obey the* Lord *your God."*

Some of what we read in the Old Testament's prophetic literature is simply preaching. It can be condemning or it can be tender, but it will always be probing, insightful and hard to ignore. There is also uplifting poetry—the raw material for worship. But we also expect to find predictions about the future. Much of what we have seen so far was future to Zechariah and his generation, and we can track with satisfaction how history developed as the prophet said it would. Some of what we read is future to us as well, having yet to be fulfilled. Chapter 6 falls into that category.

Most of us are both fascinated and a little fearful about what might be in our future. Some time ago the

Fortune Book Club promoted a featured book entitled *The Great Boom Ahead*. It claims to be "your comprehensive guide to personal and business profit in the new era of prosperity." With flourish the book club adds,

> A must read book! The upbeat message and breakthrough tools individuals and businesses need to get our economy moving again. . . . The Dow plummets to lows in the range of 1700 to 2350 between the summer of 1993 and the spring or fall of 1994, then streaks to 7000 to 8500 between 2006 and 2010. Mortgage rates fall to 5 to 6 percent by mid-1998. There is little or no inflation over the coming 20 years, despite dramatic economic growth. Those are just a few of Harry Dent's astonishing economic forecasts.[1]

The author predicted that the United States will come screaming out of recession and slow growth into the biggest upswing in history, and then he tells you how to profit from the coming boom. There are recommendations about your portfolio, about methods for organizing your company to take full advantage of the booming economy. Anticipating the great boom ahead is a refreshing antidote for the current gloom and doom economic scenario. It makes you want to go right out and spend $16.95 so you can imbibe such optimism.

That review takes up most of the page. But there was a little box on the bottom that has some other books of economic forecasts that may be of interest. The first one is *Bankruptcy 1995*. "This book explains the dire economic emergency facing the United States today and measures we must take to avoid total devastation."[2] By now we are sure that the first one was right (except in details), and the second one was a laughable mistake. Our future is secure! Ironically, we still suppress an anxiety about losing it all.

The sixth chapter of Zechariah also portrays two future scenarios, the first one is full of foreboding images, the second one a bright picture of a new and just ruler and an age of harmony. Unlike bold secular economic forecasts, both of these futures will certainly happen. It is not a matter here of choosing which one of them to believe, but it is a matter of choosing which picture you will be in. It is a pivotal choice. Zechariah's prophecies may not be as "current" as the Fortune Book Club's, nor will they sell as well. But his forecasts of the future are the ones that must have our attention if we are to be ready for what lies ahead.

The first half of chapter 6 is the last scene in Zechariah's vision. The prophet had been shown what God was doing behind the scenes. Because He cared about the things that pressed them and because they had taken new steps to faith, the Lord gave His people a vision of some of the action that they would not normally see. For those with anxious questions about what wasn't fair and about the future, He showed them His plan to live in Jerusalem again. Other scenes revealed cleansing from sin, empowerment for service and warnings to the disobedient. Then the eighth scene and the special message that follows show that the stage was set for the coming of the Lord.

Again what we read here seems obscure, as we wonder about horses and chariots and crowns. The vision is symbolic, but these symbols would have been more plain to Zechariah's congregation than to us because these were symbols out of their world. It takes some probing for us to get it.

While it is necessary for us to seek to understand all of the component pieces of the picture as best we can, we can get sidetracked in arguments over the details. The main lines, however, are clear. First of all, the chariots of judgment are ready. Second, the crown of glory is ready. And the last verse in the chapter reminds us that it is important for us to be ready too.

The Chariots of Judgment Are Ready (6:1-8)

In the first scene of the vision, the angelic riders brought from their world-ranging perspective the bad news that the political powers of the day, the institutionalized incarnations of evil, were securely in place. The powers that had crushed God's people were impossible to budge, and they were not likely to give any concessions to the weak remnant of a once proud nation. In this last scene, the servants of the Lord are riding chariots. They are not now just messengers, but warriors, going out from "the presence of the Lord of the whole world."

That last line is an important revelation. He does not want to be seen as a private God, kept in a sacred place where His people go to meet Him (in "His house" as we say), and from whose presence they go out into the world, as if they were on their own out there. He does not just give His attention to devout Christian people as if their private relationship was

His exclusive interest, while He lets the rest of the world spin off into godless chaos. That is what a lot of folks would like us to believe. "You can do your God thing in your nice church," they tell us, "but don't bring your religion to work with you, or to the formation of school policy, or to the political arena, or to my freedom to choose what I want to do. Your religion is your private business. So keep it that way!"

The angel guide called Him "the Lord of the whole world." That can create some conflicts for God's discouraged people. If He is the Lord of the whole world, how can the power of the empire be so unmovable, so entrenched? If He is the Lord of the whole world, how can famine destroy whole nations in Africa? How can Serbs treat Bosnians so inhumanely and hold off all the horrified nations of the world who do not know how to intervene? How can hell empty itself of all the devils and send them to Rwanda? If He is the Lord of the whole world, how can sin run so freely in our country? If He is really the Lord of it all, how can He allow that severe hurt that has distorted my whole life? Why would He let that happen to me? When God's people are caught in such despair, they need this vision. Zechariah's people would see these chariots coming from the presence of the Lord of the whole world as vehicles of judgment. The intention to dispense justice was clear. They were eager to confront all of the wrongs.

"The one with the black horses is going toward the north country, the one with the white horses toward the west, and the one with the dappled horses toward the south" (6:6). A similar scenario appears in Revelation 6:1-8. Perhaps it is an expansion, another perspective of the same events. There the white horse is a conqueror, the red horse is violent death and the black horse is famine. The dappled or pale horse brings death by several different means. In Zechariah's landscape, all of these judgments come out into the earth from between two bronze mountains. They may be no more than apocalyptic drapery, but perhaps they are meant to reinforce the clear message that all of this comes from "the presence of the Lord of the whole world."

"When the powerful horses went out, they were straining to go throughout the earth. And he said, 'Go throughout the earth!' So they went throughout the earth" (Zechariah 6:7). If repetition is intended to underline a key phrase, this one is double underlined. The chariots of judgment went *throughout the earth*—everywhere! This is not just about a judgment on the Persians, whose regime was so oppressive and unyielding. This is more than judgment on the Jews' neighbors who made their lives so grievously difficult. This is not just judgment on the Nazis, the communists, the Dictator of the Month, your nasty supervisor or the father who abused you. The picture here is of a day when the Lord will release the chariots of judgment who will bring famine and violent death. There isn't an unbeliever out there who will not be caught in it.

But Babylon is a special case. "Those going toward the north country have given my Spirit rest. . . ." From Judea, the highway north would take you to Babylon, skirting the massive desert that lay between the two countries. So this is judgment on Babylon, the capital of the Persian Empire. But the picture is much larger than the Babylon of that day. It is only when the Babylon of the final days has fallen that God's Spirit will find His complete rest and will be fully vindicated (Revelation 19:1-5). The Lord gave us the vision because He wanted us to see that His warrior angels are straining to go, eager to deliver this judgment. The angels of God and the Spirit of God Himself are troubled by the waiting because the outcry of a wicked world is so strong. It is only because of His mercy that He waits (2 Peter 3:9). But He wants us to see that He is not at all indifferent to the injustices we suffer just because His plan to make it right has been put on pause.

In Zechariah 5, God's people were told that the curse of the scroll, the sword of Damocles, was suspended over them. Judgment begins with the house of God, all the while straining to respond to the distortions and hurt caused by sin and godlessness throughout the whole world. This is apocalyptic—it is dramatically bigger than most of us have begun to imagine. The chariots of judgment are ready. That is a message that we need to hear. It is a message that our whole world needs to hear. It is a concern to me that in many of our franchised evangelistic methods, there is no mention of the danger of sin, the wrath of God and the need for repentance.

A few years ago, I held up traffic on a side street in Oxford so that I could have my picture taken standing on a cross built into the cobblestones which commemorates the place where Hugh Latimer and Nicholas Ridley were burned at the stake. Latimer had been the bold preacher of the Reformation in England—careful when possible, outspoken when the core truths of the reformed faith were at risk.

When he was appointed Bishop of Worcester by Henry VIII in 1535, Latimer had to borrow from the queen a sum equal to his annual income in order to pay the king his expected advance on the first year's income—from his diocese—as a "first fruits" gift to the Supreme Head of the Church of England. It was a challenge for him to stay on the right side of such a mercurial monarch. Sometimes he chose to stand on principle instead of on political expediency, for which he was confined to the "Tower" more than once.

It was also customary for the bishops to give gifts to the king on New Year's Day—usually a purse of gold. On one of these occasions, Latimer went with his brethren to pay his respects bearing a special gift. Instead of gold though, he had brought a copy of the New Testament, with a page folded down to this passage: "Whoremongers and adulterers God will judge" (Hebrews 13:4, KJV).[3] Everybody (even the Supreme Head of the Church of England) needs to hear the message of judgment when he or she chooses to live above the law of God and its judgments. For some, this is a message of encouragement that God will make wrong things right. For others, it stands as a warning that must not be trivialized or disregarded.

Jesus delivered the same message in a story to which the oppressed people of Galilee could relate. He said,

> As you are going with your adversary to the magistrate, try hard to be reconciled to him on the way, or he may drag you off to the judge, and the judge turn you over to the officer, and

> the officer throw you into prison. I tell you, you will not get out until you have paid the last penny. (Luke 12:58-59)

The chariots of judgment are ready, and they are straining to be released to restore justice and fairness by pouring out God's judgment on the world. There may still be time for plea bargaining, but best you look after it before His chariots of judgment are released upon a wicked world.

> God was reconciling the world to himself in Christ, not counting men's sins against them. And he has committed to us the message of reconciliation. We are therefore Christ's ambassadors, as though God were making his appeal through us. We implore you on Christ's behalf: Be reconciled to God. (2 Corinthians 5:19-20)

The Crown of Glory Is Ready (6:9-15)

We have come to the end of the vision, but what happens next is almost an extension of it. It is as if the Lord confirmed the vision with a message that was given to the prophet in a different way.

"The word of the LORD came to me," it says (6:9). We're not told how it came, but prophetic messages were received as specific and trustworthy words from the Lord. Again the word to Zechariah came illustrated to make sure the point registered. The Lord took the initiative to give His man a message of hope. It is something He wanted His people to hear.

In fact, the Lord gave him instructions for a dramatic play. Much of the content of this message had already been delivered in chapter 2, when the Lord promised to come back to live in Jerusalem. But now the same word comes in another medium, confirming the vision and the beautiful piece of Hebrew poetry that followed it. The repetition of the message, in yet another form, reinforced the importance of what the Lord had to say.

It was already an important occasion. Some prominent Jews had arrived from Babylon with a gift of silver and gold for the temple project.

The previous September the prophet Haggai had stood up and said, "You have started the building project, and now I have another word from the Lord for you." We can envision him asking, "Is there anyone here who can remember the previous temple?" A few old-timers raised their hands. The prophet continued, "How does this look to you?" What they were building looked like cinder block construction compared to the beautiful stones that Solomon had quarried at great expense. He said, "It doesn't look like much, does it?" It seems he touched the discouragement they were feeling. How could this ever be anything worth doing? "Let me say this: Be strong, Zerubbabel and be strong, Joshua. Keep doing it because I am with you and my Spirit remains among you. It doesn't matter if it is small because, I am in this!" (see Haggai 2:1-5). Zechariah's similar word for Zerubbabel had been, "Who despises the day of small things?" (Zechariah 4:10). He encouraged great joy among them as they worked.

Then Haggai made a prediction that was hard to believe: "This is what the Lord Almighty says: 'In a little while, I will once more shake the heavens and the earth, the sea and the dry land. I will shake all nations, and the desired of all nations will come, and I will fill this house with glory' " (Haggai 2:6-7). This place will be spectacularly endowed with the wealth of the nations. It may not look like it now, but if you just keep doing what you are doing in obedience and faith, the Lord will pay for the project before it is finished.

> "The silver is mine, and the gold is mine," declares the LORD Almighty. "The glory of this present house will be greater than the glory of the former house," says the LORD Almighty. "And in this place I will grant peace." (2:8-9)

What encouraging news! The work on the temple continued, though they could hardly imagine how it would be finished in that kind of style. Perhaps the preacher was just especially enthusiastic today!

Then within months Heldai, Tobijah and Jedaiah brought a large gift from the exiles who were still in Babylon. And it was gold and silver—the very materials that would give their building a touch of class. What a tremendous boost! What an answer to the specific prophecy of Haggai! The rest of that prophecy was fulfilled years later when an impostor of a Jewish king named Herod tried to secure his acceptance by spending a fortune and forty years to reconstruct and lavishly redecorate that building until it really was more magnificent than Solomon's.

Zechariah was instructed to go to the house of Josiah, where he would find these men from Babylon to formally receive their gifts.

The word from the Lord that follows is obscure at first, launching from the immediate occasion to a prophetic scenario that reaches into a distant future when the reign of God will be restored.

"Take the silver and gold and make a crown, and set it on the head of the high priest, Joshua son of Jehozadak" (Zechariah 6:11). That seems like a rather extravagant use of this costly contribution. Gold and silver would nicely replenish their treasury. It could be used to furnish the building more grandly than they could otherwise afford. Imagine gold-plated doors and silver gates. Imagine gold columns and silver utensils. They could devise many uses for gold and silver.

But the Lord specifically directed that they use it to make a crown for Joshua. The word "crown" in Hebrew is oddly plural, and perhaps we are meant to imagine a multi-tiered crown, as if many crowns were fashioned into one. It would be quite ornate. You might say they "crowned him with many crowns." If it seemed a little overdone, in view of the poverty of the project, it is important to seek the sense of the symbolism here. Why did the Lord direct that the contribution was to go for a spectacular crown for the high priest?

Joshua was invited to come and be part of the drama that would illustrate a prophetic message. "This is what the LORD Almighty says: 'Here is the man whose name is the Branch . . ." (6:12).

The promises of the Branch and the temple

There are six Messianic promises built into this little drama. First of all, the promise of "the Branch" is renewed. A king from the line of David would come to rule over them in a new age. Second, "he will branch out from his place" (6:12). He is what He is by nature—He will not be a product of His times. It is as if He will come from somewhere else. Third, He will "build the temple of the LORD" (6:12). It is said twice for emphasis, and we should expect it then to be fulfilled literally. The reference was not to the current simple structure being built, but to another temple and another temple builder like this man Joshua who stood before them as a symbol of the Branch yet to come.

The Temple Institute in Israel today has been raising funds for several years and collecting materials to build the temple anticipating the Messiah's arrival. Many of the pieces of equipment and the articles of clothing for the priests have already been fabricated, using the descriptions in Leviticus and Ezekiel for direction. Of special interest are the menorah and other major pieces that will be made of pure gold. Even though they do not know what to do about the current tenants on the Temple Mount, there are Jewish people who believe this prophecy of Zechariah will be fulfilled literally when the Messiah comes.[4] In the text it is underscored: When He comes, He will build His temple.

The promises of the ruler, the priest and the Gentiles

The fourth promise is that He "will sit and rule on his throne" (6:13). He will not merely be the Healer of our hurts, the cosmic servant who exists to satisfy our needs and wants. He comes as the ruler. Fifth, "he will be a priest on his throne" (6:13). The priest was the one who dealt with their sin. The king was their leader. This one would come to be both. The Messiah King would also be their priest. So this plural crown is the priest's tiara and king's royal crown fashioned into one. Sixth, "those who are far away will come and help build the temple of the LORD" (6:15). People "far away" was a Jewish slur for Gentiles. They were considered to be so far from God that they were beyond hope. But even they are included in this prophecy.[5]

Those who were gathered in Josiah's house that day would know that all of that wasn't about Joshua, their high priest, though he would have been honored to be cast in that role. When Zechariah was finished, the crown was given to Heldai, Tobijah, Jedaiah and Hen, their host's brother, so that they could deposit it in the temple. It was to be a reminder, a memorial of this prophecy, and it was to wait there for the priest/king Messiah to come and claim it as His own. They were prepared for His arrival with the crown of glory waiting for Him. The prophecy had said that the Jewish people would recognize Him when He came, and they would know that God had sent Him. Imagine that! Many of the Jewish people did not recognize Him the first time He came to them. But later in this book, Zechariah will predict that when Jesus comes again, they will recognize Him and will be overcome with mourning, because they will see Him as the One they have pierced (12:10).

The chariots of judgment are ready. The crown of glory is ready. The Lord showed Himself to them to be ready and eager to come. They were making themselves ready by preparing His crown, eager that He should come and reign as their great High Priest and King.

The French Revolution was a massive revolt against the pompous monarchy, against the rule of aristocrats and their blood-sucking opulent lifestyle. The people of France rid themselves of kings and queens—it was a new era. France's experiment in republican government, however, did not get off to a good start, for the repressed anger of many generations erupted into unprecedented violence, blood and anarchy. Then Citizen Bonaparte emerged from the ranks of the army of commoners. In him the revolutionaries had a hero who could bring peace to the land and make the great ideals of liberty, equality and fraternity prevail, perhaps throughout the whole world. The people of France made him Consul for Life. It was Bonaparte himself, known to the world as Napoleon, who decided to make himself emperor.

It was a big show, the major event of the turn of a new century, with Pope Pius VII designated to bless him and put the crown on his head. When countless dignitaries were assembled and the grand proceedings brought them all to that moment when the Pope stood before the man of the hour with the crown in his hands, Napoleon magisterially reached for it and, in a gesture understood by all who were there, put the crown on his head himself.[6]

Many others before and after him have tried to crown themselves, though perhaps with more subtlety. In our system it tends to be politicians who promise more than anybody could ever deliver. But there isn't anybody who can wear that crown except Jesus Christ. One day He will step back into the scene of history. He will direct the chariots of judgment to the four corners of the earth giving the aggrieved Spirit of the Lord the satisfaction of justice. Then He will take that many-tiered crown and everyone will know that the Lord Almighty has sent Him. It is not a remote possibility. It is a "word of the Lord." The chariots of judgment are ready, and the crown of glory is ready.

The Last Line Is Worth a Careful Look

The chapter closes with, "This will happen if you diligently obey the LORD your God" (6:15).

There is Messianic fervor among some Jews today. In recent years the followers of the remarkable Rabbi Menachem Schneerson, the aged and venerated leader of the ultra-orthodox Lubavitcher movement headquartered in Brooklyn, had been earnestly praying that God would certify Schneerson to be the Jewish Messiah. His death left them without a strong candidate, but the longing for a messiah is a theme that has persisted in the experience of the Jews for centuries.[7]

In the sixteenth century, the Spanish Inquisition forced resident Jews to either convert to Christianity or to leave the country. There were not many places to go, but some made their way to Palestine. Their descendants can be found in ancient Jewish communities like Safed in the Galilee. They came back to the land to wait for the Messiah, taking literally the instruction, "If you diligently obey, I will come to you." These very devout people believe that the Messiah will come on a Sabbath day, so they get up every Saturday morning hoping and longing that that will be the day. When the sun goes down and the Messiah has not arrived, they look at each other with mourning and conclude, "There must be sin in our lives." They spend some time in meditation and remorse, and then they try to live another week in more diligent obedience so that the Messiah will be free to come.[8]

There is a better reading of this verse. The intention here is to say that you will be in the picture in the second half of this chapter if you are a follower of the Lord. The alternative is that you will be in the first picture—the picture of judgment. Both will happen. What is pivotal here is not what will make Him come, but which picture you will be in.

Unfortunately verse 15 has often been misapplied, leading to a preoccupation with following the law. This insistence became the driving theme of Ezra's work—the establishment of the Law as their guide (Ezra 7:10). The Pharisees eventually emerged out of that back-to-God movement, but they had so lost their original purpose that when the Messiah did come to remove the sin of the land in a single day, not only did they not recognize that the Lord Almighty had sent Him, but they became the leaders of a coalition to get rid of Him.[9]

Their counterparts in our time are good people who call themselves Christians and think they are in the second picture of this chapter when really they are not—their religion is just empty words and perfunctory obedience. The challenge in the last line here is to recognize Him now. That is the purpose of this prophetic disclosure. Come to Him as your Priest—let Him take care of your sins with His work of deep cleansing. Come to Him as your King—follow Him closely and diligently. Both of those roles come together as you crown Him with both crowns. Then when the next temple project gets underway, you will be included in the grandest era of history as the Lord Jesus Christ rebuilds the world that He has purged of sin and evil.

My grandfather homesteaded a farm near Hawarden, Saskatchewan in 1906. The great empty prairies of Canada were pioneered by brave people from England, Germany, the Ukraine and elsewhere. Many had no farming experience, but they were given free land if they would live on it and work it. My grandparents came from Scotland. I remember their wonderfully thick accents. We found something beautiful and warm in being "laddies and lassies," and my grandmother's shortbread was one of life's major delights. It always seemed to me that their house was so very big and so very safe.

I remember my grandfather talking about the early days when the land was still half empty, and in the dry years they lived in fear of prairie fire. He told of a time when he saw smoke on the horizon. The conditions were right and he knew it. As quickly as he could, he hitched up his team and started cutting furrows around the home place in hopes he could cut enough width to prevent the inferno from jumping the fire break.

I listened with wide-eyed wonder. It was not hard for my six-year-old imagination to picture a fire on that land that stretched on forever. And I could, without fear, imagine the devastating flames and the smoke, because we were sitting secure in that wonderful, solid, big old farm house that I thought would always stand strong.

The chariots of judgment are real. But so is the coronation. We can anticipate the judgment without fear if we are also ready for the return of the King.

The force of the messages of the sixth chapter is to encourage us to come into the security of Jesus' love and acceptance, to acknowledge Him as our Priest, letting Him take care of our sin, to acknowledge Him as our King, yielding our lives to Him now. The stage is set for His coming: The chariots of judgment are ready, the crown of glory is ready. Now let's you and me be ready!

Discussion Questions for Further Study

1. What fearful things may be in your future? What can you anticipate with firm hope?
2. Read through Revelation 6 and note some of what the world will experience when the horses of the Apocalypse are released.
3. If Jesus' crown is to be multi-tiered, what are some of the realms over which He will be crowned King?
4. Picture Jesus as "Priest on His throne." He is there to help you to find God. Picture Jesus as "clothed with majesty . . . and ru[ling] on his throne." He is sovereign over all. In what ways do these pictures help you to know how to approach Him?

Endnotes

[1] Fortune Book Club newsletter, January 1993.
[2] Ibid.

3 Paul Lee Tan, "Courageous Gift to Henry VIII," *Encyclopedia of 7,700 Illustrations: Signs of the Times* (Rockville, MD: Assurance Publishers, 1979), 114; and Clara Stuart, *Latimer* (Grand Rapids: Zondervan, 1986).

4 "In the Jewish Quarter of Jerusalem there is a group of young Levites who are currently studying the temple scrolls, preparing themselves for the day when the Temple will be rebuilt, and the sacrificial system reinstituted.

"Elsewhere in Jerusalem there are rabbis and scholars who are researching, dreaming, and planning for the rebuilding of the Temple. Plans have actually been drawn and funds are being raised.

"At the Temple Institute in Jerusalem, established by Rabbi Israel Ariel, visitors to Jerusalem see temple vessels, clothing, and furnishings that have been prepared for actual use when the Temple has been rebuilt. These items have been made in exacting detail of the original temple vessels and furnishings. The Institute has already completed 53 of the 103 vessels required for temple worship.

"They have also completed the High Priest's garments and the breast-plate. Each stone in the breast-plate was carefully set, as Scripture and rabbinic tradition dictate. The temple laver can also be seen, along with the instruments used for sacrifice. Rabbi Ariel is currently trying to raise funds so the Institute can make an authentic "Menorah" (seven-branch candelabrum). The cost of such a project is in the millions of dollars.

"Also on display at the Temple Institute are biblical harps which were used by the Levitical priests in singing and chanting the 'Songs of Ascent' and other melodies during times of worship, praise, prayer, and sacrifice.

"More recently, the Institute has been searching the nations of the world for a particular breed of cattle with color resembling the Talmudic description of the 'red heifer.' According to the Scriptures, the ashes of the 'red heifer' were needed to provide cleansing for the instruments and individuals working on or within the Temple (see Numbers 19:1-22). . . . It is the hope and prayer of Rabbi Ariel and others that by the time the 'red heifer' has been bred, the new Temple will be standing. It can then be dedicated to God" (Harold A. Sovener, "The Temple: Where Did It Stand? Where Will It Be Rebuilt? Part II," *The Chosen People*, Dec. 92, 14).

[5] Walter C. Kaiser, Jr., *Micah-Malachi*, The Communicator's Commentary, vol. 21 (Dallas, TX: Word Books, 1992), 347.

[6] "Napoleon I," *The New Columbia Encyclopedia* (New York: Columbia University Press, 1975), 1178-1179.

[7] Charitey Simmons, "Hasidim Adjust to Rabbi's Death," *The Christian Century*, January 4, 1995, 6-7.

[8] From a tape recording of the author's visit in a synagogue in Safed in March 1979.

[9] The Jewish leaders who opposed Jesus in the end were usually described as "the chief priests [who would have been of the Sadducees] and the elders" (Matthew 26:3, 47, 57; 27:1, 3, 12, 20, 41; 28:12). The Pharisees are only specifically mentioned as included in the sponsorship of the arresting party (John 18:3). Apparently when the matter became a formal process, they were not the ones holding the reigns of power. There can be no doubt, however, that their formal legalism was considered a spiritual death trap by Jesus (Matthew 23).

Part 2

The Way Things Ought to Be

7

The Question of Fasting

Zechariah 7:1-14

In the fourth year of King Darius, the word of the LORD came to Zechariah on the fourth day of the ninth month, the month of Kislev. The people of Bethel had sent Sharezer and Regem-Melech, together with their men, to entreat the LORD by asking the priests of the house of the LORD Almighty and the prophets, "Should I mourn and fast in the fifth month, as I have done for so many years?"

Then the word of the LORD Almighty came to me: "Ask all the people of the land and the priests, 'When you fasted and mourned in the fifth and seventh months for the past seventy years, was it really for me that you fasted? And when you were eating and drinking, were you not just feasting for yourselves? Are these not the words the LORD proclaimed through the earlier prophets when Jerusalem and its surrounding towns were at rest and prosperous, and the Negev and the western foothills were settled?' "

And the word of the LORD came again to Zechariah: "This is what the LORD Almighty says: 'Administer true justice; show mercy and compassion to one an-

other. Do not oppress the widow or the fatherless, the alien or the poor. In your hearts do not think evil of each other.'

"But they refused to pay attention; stubbornly they turned their backs and stopped up their ears. They made their hearts as hard as flint and would not listen to the law or to the words that the LORD Almighty had sent by his Spirit through the earlier prophets. So the LORD Almighty was very angry.

" 'When I called, they did not listen; so when they called, I would not listen,' says the LORD Almighty. 'I scattered them with a whirlwind among all the nations, where they were strangers. The land was left so desolate behind them that no one could come or go. This is how they made the pleasant land desolate.' "

Haggai called for a return to the formal service of Judah's covenant God. Zechariah called for a return to service from the heart. The great vision of chapters 1-6 called for a revival of faith, a revival of holiness, a revival of Spirit filling and a revival of anticipation. With the developments of chapter 7, the prophet now calls for a revival of worship.

What was the *heart* motive behind their religious service? Was it really for God? (7:5). Did they have *hearts* of mercy and compassion? (7:9). In their *hearts* they were not to think evil of each other (7:10). They were reminded of their forefathers who made their *hearts* as hard as flint and would not listen (7:12).

People came from Bethel with a question about the order of worship, and in response the prophet raised several questions about what was in their hearts when they came to worship. It is a very special revival sermon that we need to hear, a cogent message about the way things ought to be.

Let's pick up Judah's story. In the fourth year of Darius, things looked a lot better for the Jewish community. They had been living with a lot of grief from their neighbors to the north, but all of that had been decisively shut down by a decree from the king of Persia himself, who not only said, "Leave them alone down there," but also, "Send them everything they may requisition for their project." It was a wonderful and clearly providential development, chronicled by Ezra years later (Ezra 6:6-12). The building project was moving along. They had been at it for two years, and it was time to begin planning the dedication celebration. After all this time, it was actually going to happen! The date was the fourth of Kislev or, on our Julian calendar, the seventh of December, 518 B.C.

But how could they wholeheartedly celebrate anything when the ethos of their national identity was filled with tragedy?

August 9 was a day that lived in infamy for these people. It was the anniversary of the day that God told the Israelites they would have to stay in the desert another forty years because of their unbelief. And they remembered. It was also the day in 587 B.C. when Jerusalem fell to Nebuchadnezzar and was totally destroyed. Double infamy. They lived with those memories and commemorated the day with sorrow. Then as if providence conspired to teach them a dark lesson never to be forgotten, August 9 was the day the Romans demolished the second temple in 70 A.D. One more: It was August 9 in 135 when the Romans destroyed Jerusalem for the second time, and General

Turnus Rufus literally ran a plow over the ruins of the temple, specifically fulfilling the prophecy of Micah who said that the destruction would be so complete that you could plant a field there. Even after only two of these national tragedies, August 9 was a day of solemn remembrance and regrets.[1]

The Old Testament required an annual solemn fast day—Yom Kippur, the Day of Atonement—when God's people mourned for sin and repented with a formal sacrifice. They were commanded to deny themselves as they observed this holy occasion. Fasting was to them a sign of intense prayer and mourning. So it would have been a natural development for the Jews in exile to add four more fasting days to their calendar to mourn their past. The fast of the tenth month fell on the tenth of Tebeth, which was the day when the king of Babylon laid siege to Jerusalem. The fast of the fourth month was on the ninth of Tammuz, the day when the city walls were breached. The fast of the fifth month, the ninth of Ab (August 9) was when the house of God was destroyed by fire. And the fast of the seventh month was on the third day of Tishri, the anniversary of the assassination of Gedaliah.[2]

It appears that there were some who wondered if their penance had been acted out long enough. Must they forevermore live with such memories of their national sorrows? Some came down from Bethel, twelve miles to the north, to raise the question. The leaders of the group had Babylonian names, indicating that they were children of the exile, born in that foreign land, younger people who were tired of living with the grief of their parents and grandparents, tired of hearing about the depression, impatient to get on with rebuilding their national existence without the impediment of all those bad memories.

"Can't we drop some of our days of mourning? Days of fasting make us feel bad. If you don't feel bad at the beginning of the day, doing without food will surely make you feel bad by the end of it. It has been sixty-eight years now since the destruction of the temple. Jeremiah said that we will live with grief for seventy years. We have acted that out with fast days all these years. The temple project is nearing completion. Can we be done with fast days and national mourning now? Can we drop these fasts when we rededicate the building?"

It says they came to entreat the Lord—to "stroke the face of God." They came to pray, and the priests and the prophets, those who speak for God, gathered in a special council to consider this question and to give them an answer from the Lord. Can we expect the promised blessing now and get on with it? Have we done what we need to do to prove that we are sorry and to earn the promised blessings?

In the middle of that meeting, Zechariah stood up with a special insight—the word of the Lord Almighty that came to him for that occasion and for that question. It was a prophetic gift of vision to see the heart of the issue, to probe to a deeper level, to take them beyond the form to the substance of the matter, beyond the "what" question to the "why," to expose the motives of those who would argue that the fasts be observed, as well as the motives of those who petitioned for them to be discontinued. And it came in the form of a probing intrusive question:

> Then the word of the LORD Almighty came to me: "Ask all the people of the land and the priests, 'When you fasted and mourned in the fifth and seventh months for the past seventy years, was it really for me that you fasted?' " (7:4-5)

He is addressing the whole assembly now. "You all know how easy it is to enjoy feast days. We treat ourselves to the blessing of God when we eat together. If we want a quorum at the annual meeting, we serve food. Many more people come when we feast than when we fast, because we like it. We do it for ourselves and we enjoy it."

The irony is that this is the message of the earlier prophets. (In fact, these two chapters of Zechariah are a succinct summary of the main themes of all of the preaching prophets.) It's a shallow religious observance that is motivated only by what you get out of it. An earlier generation lost the land, which they had called "the Pleasant Land," because while they were doing their religious exercises, they were still living for themselves. And it did not matter that they kept that sacrifice going and did all of the fasting and the things that God required. They lost the land! They lost His presence! They lost the blessing because they refused to go any deeper. When they fasted, was it really for God? Or did they only go through the religious forms of their tradition, hoping to gain something to add to their self-centered pursuits?

Each generation has its own form of selfishness. We all need the prophet's challenge. What follows in verses 9 and 10 are four commandments for the cultivation of a selfless spirit. The Lord will ask His prophet to call us up short, but He will also go on to show us another way.

These simple commandments are major themes in Isaiah and Hosea, and they are almost a direct quote from the prophet Micah (Micah 6:8). By recalling familiar material, Zechariah reminded them again that perhaps it was not time to omit annually observed contemplations of their national tragedies because they had yet to learn the lessons of their history.

> This is what the LORD Almighty says: "Administer true justice; show mercy and compassion to one another. Do not oppress the widow or the fatherless, the alien or the poor. In your hearts do not think evil of each other." (Zechariah 7:9-10)

Or you could say, "Be fair, be generous, be sensitive and be care-full."

"Administer True Justice"—Be Fair (7:9)

We all have an instinct for what is straight, what is true, what is right. We sense it most clearly when we are the ones who have been wronged. But it seems that our general sense of what is right has been diluted by spending a lifetime in a world where so much is not right that wrong begins to be normal.

There is a sign on a busy Chicago expressway that says, "To turn left, make two right turns." That's not very helpful when you are in the left lane in six lanes of city traffic! Instructions like that may be normal in Chicago. It may have seemed right and normal to the engineer who designed it, but it doesn't help the tourist passing at fifty-five miles an hour. In our twisted world, two rights often must serve to make a left because a simple left is not always available.

The prophet is saying, "Administer true justice. Do what you can to make the world fair for everyone." It is hard for us to discern what was unfair in their justice, but we do know that Nehemiah came down hard on them for economic exploitation (Nehemiah 5). And we can get a sense of the commandment by looking at the failure of justice and fairness around us. We no longer look for the truth to be established. Instead we seek the best deal we can get, and the pursuit of fairness is lost in the pursuit of advantage.

Children are less sophisticated about all of this than we are. When we grow up, we mask our cruelty in a certain sophistication, but we can learn about ourselves by watching our children. Our feisty firstborn at age four would complain if she felt that her younger brother and sister were being given some preferential treatment. Her line was, "That's not fair to me! It's not fair to me!" We adults, in the same situation, would simply object that it was not fair, leaving off the personal reference. We should be so honest as our children! The fact is that our sense of fairness is not so finely tuned to what is fair or good for everybody else as it is tuned to what is good for me. That is how we measure justice.

But true justice rises above personal considerations because it is blind to personal advantage, or at least it supersedes it. In 1975 in Sulphur Springs, Louisiana, municipal judge E.W. Thompson came into court late with an apology, explaining that he was stopped by a policeman for driving forty-two miles per hour in a "maximum thirty" zone. He proceeded with the order of business and before the docket was complete, his own name came up. To the wonderment of those in the room, he stood up, took off his robe, went down to stand in front of the bar and pleaded guilty. He then returned to the dais, put on his robe, sat down, pounded the gavel on the desk and ordered, "Seventeen dollars and fifty cents." The law must apply to all.[3]

True justice is not fudged just for you. We Christians may be lured into believing that is the case because God so freely and graciously forgives us. But in our world of diluted justice, we are not always aware of what it cost God to do that. He is perfectly just. He faithfully forgives us our sins. But more precisely, "he is faithful and *just* and will forgive us our sins" (1 John 1:9, emphasis added). He does not sacrifice His justice when He forgives us, and we must be careful not to lose our sense of that justice—a standard above self-interest.

Brutus is familiar to us as the friend of Julius Caesar who aided in the assassination of his friend. "You too, Brutus?" Caesar cried out on his deathbed.[4] But there was another side of this man of which we do not hear. Brutus was elected to be one of the last Consuls in the Roman Republic before the great civil war. During those turbulent days there was a man named Tarquin who led a conspiracy to overthrow the government and install himself as king. Brutus found himself to be the judge presiding over the trial of those who were drawn into this treasonous conspiracy. Before him stood Tarquin. Other conspirators were brought in, and to his utter horror he discovered that two of the men at the heart of the conspiracy were his own sons. Understand that familial affection in Rome was among the highest of their values. One's loyalty to family was stronger than one's loyalty to truth.

As his sons were brought in, people in the crowd felt the tension, and they cried out to him with tears to have mercy on his sons. But the character of the judge was revealed in the moment of crisis. When it came time to pound the gavel on that desk, Brutus ordered his sons to be beheaded in his presence. The ancient author who tells us this story concludes by saying, "He ceased to be a father, that he might execute the duties of a Consul, and choose to live childless rather than to neglect the public punishment of a crime."[5]

When the prophet said, "Administer true justice," he called the Jewish people to rise above their selfish instincts and interests and to make the world fair for somebody else. It is a difficult, unnatural step, but it is the beginning of the remission of the malignancy of selfishness.

"Show Mercy and Compassion"—Be Generous (7:9)

Second, God commanded His people to show mercy. "Mercy" is a soft word in English. Most commonly it means that for no reason we withhold giving harsh treatment to someone who surely deserves it. At best it means that I am being good to you though I have every right to give you something bad. But the Hebrew word is *hesed*, a strong word often translated in the Psalms "loving-kindness," or in newer translations, "covenant love." It has a strong positive content, an intentional loyalty and commitment with genuine feeling of selfless love.

The best analogy to define what is commanded here is the Lord's love for His chosen people. But He knows that sometimes we need something closer to our own experience before we understand that, and so He directed Hosea to marry a woman who would scandalously leave him for a life of sin. Hosea's love for Gomer becomes our picture of *hesed*—love with a commitment. And that is what we are commanded to practice.

It was clear to Hosea that the Lord had specifically given this young woman to him to be his wife. Her name rang with loveliness in the ears of a Hebrew man, reminiscent of a familiar flower. But there may have been some foreboding from the beginning that this was not going to be a happy story.

The names of their children rang with double meaning, the prophet's message mirrored in their family life. Their firstborn was a son that God told him to name Jezreel, a reminder to his people that they would reap the bitter fruit of Jehu's massacre at Jezreel. And Hosea would wonder what was in the future for him and his family. The second child was a daughter, named by the Lord's direction Lo-Ruhamah, which means "not loved." She bore the chilling message that the strong bonds of heartfelt love between the Lord and His people were no longer there. God was expressing His hurt and Hosea shared that hurt as he had to admit, at least to himself, that there was no longer any love in his marriage either. The third was a boy, given the prophetic name Lo-

Ammi, which means "not mine." With that, the Lord mournfully released His people to go their own way. Hosea felt the Lord's grief as he recognized that Gomer's child was not his, and he released his lovely young wife to a life of temple prostitution (Hosea 1-2).

His children were his sermon illustrations. He would stand up on the temple steps and say, "You know that my family life has been a tragedy. But the word of the Lord is that our covenant has become a tragedy too. Where is the love, the *hesed*, the commitment, the feeling, the promise, the loyalty? It's not there anymore, is it?" The prophet's anguish at losing his wife is the picture of the heart of God when the tenderness and binding love that should have come back from His people had slipped away as they picked up other pursuits. "There is no faithfulness, no *hesed*, no acknowledgment of God in the land. . . . For I desired *hesed*, not sacrifice, and acknowledgment of God rather than burnt offerings" (4:1; 6:6).

Using that same powerful word, *hesed*, Zechariah came back to the people again and said, "It is not enough just to do all of your good, religious things, whether it is fasting or celebrating. What the Lord wants is your loyalty love! Come back to that!"

He went on to tell them they were to show that love to one another as well. This time the word is translated "compassion," and it is a construction on the Hebrew word for a woman's womb. It contains a feeling that is strongly maternal. There is a profound connecting bond between the mother and her unborn child, an unspoken commitment to nurture and protect, a visceral sense that the future of the mother is bound up in the future of the child. There is nothing more important to her than the well-being of that baby. The Lord is saying, "I want you to give that kind of concern to those around you. Renew your capacity for that in your *hesed* bond with Me, then go out and give it to others. As I have been generous with you, you are now free and commissioned to be generous with all." It is called "compassion," and it is perfectly selfless. It is the picture of Hosea buying back his wife at the slave auction after her life of immorality (Hosea 3). Given as an alternative to the people's pattern of doing the good things they did for what they got out of it, this commandment offered an alternative focus, asking them to disregard their own needs and immerse themselves in the needs of others. God was asking them, "Can you do this for Me?"

"Do Not Oppress the Widow"—Be Sensitive (7:10)

There was no Social Security safety net in Judah. Before our twentieth-century political movements that said that the government can do it and before the "social gospel" that said that social service *is* the gospel, Christians were very good at looking after people with special needs. The early Church provided the Roman world with hospitals. In the Middle Ages, monastic houses were centers of refuge and charity. In the nineteenth century, the Church provided what are now government sponsored programs.

"Do not oppress the widow or the fatherless, the alien or the poor," Zechariah said (7:10). Those listed in this verse were the weak people in society, the neediest, the disadvantaged, those with the least leverage or power. This commandment was thundered by Amos (5:21-26). It was thrust out with power by Micah (6:6-8). It was richly developed by Isaiah (56:1; 61:1-9). Zechariah is saying, "Do not oppress these people." But the wider body of prophetic literature that he is referencing demands that we take the initiative to look after the people who do not share our advantages. Do it, and you will find that it becomes for you an antidote to a selfishness that runs through your character.

John Newton, a wretch of a slave who became a slave trader that the Lord saved, gave us the hymn "Amazing Grace," became a preacher on the east end of London and joined his friend William Wilberforce in the movement to abolish slavery in the British empire.[6] The antislavery movement was driven by Christians out of their compassion for those who were disadvantaged and had no power of their own. William Booth had a remarkable experience of God, founded the Salvation Army and spent his life fishing people out of the gutter, dealing forcefully with their alcoholism and their personal needs while seeking God to give them a fresh start spiritually.[7] All of that came from a heart for God and a life of self-forgetfulness. A.B. Simpson founded an independent church in New York City that spawned many ministries of compassion to the hungry people on the streets, to the young women of Manhattan who were caught in the enervating cycle of prostitution, to those who needed a temporary quiet home where they could seek the Lord to heal their physical needs, and to the people of many nations who were disadvantaged by having no opportunity to hear of the liberating life-changing gospel of Christ.[8] Special care for those with special needs is a recurring commandment.

Zechariah preached it as a call to live selflessly, to return to religion of the heart.

"Do Not Think Evil"—Be Care-full (7:10)

The fourth commandment in the sequence follows the pattern of considering others: "In your hearts do not think evil of each other." Some translations read, "Do not plot evil against your neighbor," and the commandment certainly would include that. But "do not think evil" covers more territory. It includes the two women whose feud was poisoning the church but who could not remember how it all started before the "thinking evil of one another" took over. It includes Saul's thinking being twisted by his jealousy of David so that his most loyal servant somehow became the target of his paranoia and his last years were wasted trying to kill him. Of course the counterpoint in the story is David's refusal to think evil of Saul, even though the pressure of his fugitive existence led him to feign insanity, fudge the truth to save his skin and occasionally despair of emerging from that nightmare at all. Even when he had opportunity, he refused to touch or even to disrespect that miserable shell of a man. David looked at him with sadness, acknowledging with his men the tragedy of what Saul had become, but insisting, "He is still God's man, and for that I must treat him with special respect" (see 1 Samuel 24:6).

Zechariah is saying, "God wants you to treat other people around you like that. Do not let your thinking about any of them be distorted by the evil inclinations that spring up from the contaminated soil of your hearts." Jesus impatiently told His disciples to allow the children to come to Him because they were precious to Him. The challenge for us is to consider the "little people" in our lives, whoever they may be—especially those with whom we may be at variance—and to acknowledge that even these are precious to God. It is a commandment that runs counterflow to our self-seeking impulses and our drive for self-fulfillment.

A Warning from History

Then Zechariah reminded them that this message had been rejected before and that the results had been disastrous. God had called them to a life of fairness, generosity, sensitivity and care-fullness:

> But they refused to pay attention; stubbornly they turned their backs [literally, "they turned the stubborn shoulder," like an ox refusing the yoke] and stopped up their ears. They made their hearts as hard as flint and would not listen to the law or to the words that the LORD Almighty had sent by his Spirit through the earlier prophets. So the LORD Almighty was very angry. (7:11-12)

The next two verses then become a vivid first person statement:

> *"When I called, they did not listen; so when they called, I would not listen,"* says the LORD Almighty. "I scattered them . . . [and] they made the pleasant land desolate." (7:13-14, emphasis added)

The pleasant land was God's promised gift of a fruitful life. He withdrew His blessing and they lost their land.

How could the fall of Jerusalem to Nebuchadnezzar have been a surprise? We have the writings of the prophets, the forceful words of warning that came from many voices. There was regret in the Lord's tone when He reminded the grandchildren of those taken captive, "but they did not listen."

We live with the same alternate futures. Do we choose to listen to the gloomy prophets or do we prefer to hear the positive thinkers? Clearly what they did not listen to was the call to a life of justice and mercy. They were too self-absorbed, even in their religious observance.

If our nation were to crash would we be surprised? We cannot really imagine our beautiful, bountiful "pleasant" land, a nation established with such obvious providence, becoming so depopulated and desolate that you could not travel through it. Neither could they. But Zechariah was speaking to young people who were living in the ruins of that once rich life of blessing. They were still God's people. They did their religious duties, though they were less than careful to consider His guidelines for godly living. Now the question of their annual fasts emerged from their unhappy struggle, and it was an occasion to reinforce the lesson of the nation's crash: It is what is in your heart, not just how faithfully you do your spiritual exercises, that brings you either disaster or the revival promised in chapter 8. Are you really listening? Are you hearing His commandments that lead you in selfless service? Is it a service of the heart?

Each Generation Knows Selfishness

We have dignified our selfishness as a pursuit of self-esteem and self-fulfillment—self-hyphenated words that were once suspicious, now magically reborn as something good. Abraham Maslow's hierarchy of needs has become a popular model. He proposed that our needs or drives could be stacked up pyramid style, with physiological and safety needs most basic, and self-esteem and "self-actualization" on top.[9] It is true that we are selfish from bottom to top, almost entirely motivated by our own needs. But this scheme fails as a description of the way things ought to be.

The Delphic Oracle counseled, "Know yourself."[10] Shakespeare's word was, "To thine own self be true."[11] Whitman's line was, "I dote on myself, there is a lot of me and all so luscious."[12] His "Song of Myself" goes on to say, "Nothing, not God, is greater to one than one's self."[13] Hugh Hefner's credo is surely, "Indulge yourself." It is reported that when John Dillinger was asked why he robbed banks, he simply replied, "Because that's where the money is."[14] But Jesus runs countercurrent to such a deep-seated instinct when He says, "Deny yourself" (see Luke 9:23-25).

The message in the succinct responses of both Jesus and Zechariah is that it is important to sense the subtle and malignant force of selfishness in your spirit. The pursuit of self-fulfillment is an addictive myth because, as Jesus said, you can never find your life unless you choose to lose it in something else. Fulfillment can never be found by pursuing it, but only by rejecting it as a life goal. It is only a by-product of another pursuit.

Sometimes a self-centered orientation is unavoidably obvious or even obnoxiously blatant. At least it is obvious and blatant to everybody else. Do you remember Muhammad Ali at his best? He really was "the greatest," and he knew it. Before his first fight with Joe Frazier, he proclaimed:

> "There seems to be confusion. We're going to clear this confusion up on March the eighth. We're going to decide once and for all who is king. There's not a man alive who could whup me." And he jabs the air half a dozen times. "I'm too smart." He taps his head. "I'm too pretty." He lifts his head in profile, turning as a bust on a pedestal. "I am the greatest. I am the king. I should be a postage stamp. That's the only way I could get licked."[15]

It was self-promotion at its most entertaining, narcissism delightfully caricatured in the bright lights of hero-building publicity.

But our selfishness is more cultured, more refined, usually fooling even the one who owns it. Perhaps it takes some Ali exaggeration to recognize it. Consider this "Gardener's Prayer," and wonder if it is a caricature of our own:

> Oh Lord. Grant that in some way, it may rain everyday, say from about midnight until three o'clock in the morning. But, You see, it must be gentle and warm, so that it can soak in. Grant, that at the same time, it would not rain on campion, alyssum, heliathemum, lavender, and the

> others, which You in your infinite wisdom know are drought-loving plants. I will write their names on a bit of paper, if You like. And grant that the sun may shine the whole day long, but not everywhere. Not, for instance, on the spiraea or on the gentian, platain lily, and rhododendron. And not too much. Grant that there may be plenty of dew and little wind, enough worms, no plant lice and snails, no mildew, and that once a week, thin liquid manure and guano may fall from heaven. Amen.[16]

I have often wondered in the month of June what God does with the prayer of the bride who prays for great weather and the prayer of the farmer who desperately needs rain.

The prophet draws a warning from generations who lost the blessing of God because, even in their religious observance, they were serving themselves. We study revival in our prayer meetings and we are told that earnest united prayer always precedes genuine revival. That is stated so often that it is almost self-evident. But our prayers and our fasting can lead to a smug self-righteousness instead of leading to anything good. Second Chronicles 7:14 points the way to revival, but prayer is only one of four steps commanded there.

Zechariah is unrelenting: "Fasting is OK; perhaps you could even say that fasting is good. But if you ignore these matters of the heart, these deliberate exercises in selfless service, God will not hear your prayers. Your pious fasting will be inconsequential and the very calamities that your fasting commemorates will happen again, this time to you." It was routine to mourn their losses by fasting. It would have been easy to change the style of their observance from national sorrow to joyful celebration. But before they could change their mourning to joy, they were to be sure that they had learned the causes of the curse that had been their national experience and to choose a different course.

Second Chronicles 36:16, the last verse in the Hebrew Bible, demands more careful listening: "They mocked God's messengers, despised his words and scoffed at his prophets until the wrath of the LORD was aroused against his people and there was no remedy." How important it is to listen to God, eager to hear His instruction. Beware of the addictive myth of self-fulfillment and the pursuit of self-filling in your religious observance. Seek avenues of selfless service. And ask the Lord to give you ears eager to hear His voice and hearts that resonate with the pulse of these good commandments, directing us away from ourselves.

Dear Lord, how prone I am to do what I do for myself. Forgive me. I am as caught up in the trap of self-actualization as they were. I want to make sure that what I do is for You. Thank You for patiently calling me to something deeper.

Discussion Questions for Further Study

1. Try to analyze the mixed motives that you may bring to your acts of worship and service. Can you identify how much of it you do because it's good for you? How much of what you do is consciously for the pleasure of the Lord and the benefit of others?

2. Are you more inclined to attend a church feast/celebration or a church fast/prayer meeting? Why? Do you think the Lord may desire for you to change this pattern?
3. Consider the four commandments that are designed to turn around your self-orientation. Imagine one or two things you can do in obedience to each of these, and then consider how deliberately doing them would make your next week different.
   "Administer true justice"—Be fair
   "Show mercy and compassion"—Be generous
   "Do not oppress the widow"—Be sensitive
   "Do not think evil"—Be care-full
4. What warnings of judgment do you not listen to carefully enough? What do you know that you should do differently but don't change?
5. If each generation has its own form of selfishness, so do each of us. How does it show up in your life? What is the Lord saying to you about what needs to be replaced with selfless service?

Endnotes

[1] Carl Friedrich Keil, *The Twelve Minor Prophets*, trans. James Martin, Biblical Commentary on the Old Testament, vol. 11 (Grand Rapids, MI: Wm. B. Eerdmans Publishing Company, 1989), 306.

[2] Kenneth Barker, *The Expositor's Bible Commentary*, vol. 7 (Grand Rapids, MI: Zondervan Publishing House, 1985), 643, quoting *The Illustrated Family Encyclopedia* (8:93).

[3] Paul Lee Tan, "When Judge Steps Down," *Encyclopedia of 7,700 Illustrations: Signs of the Times* (Rockville, MD: Assurance Publishers, 1979), 1248-1249.

[4] William Shakespeare, "Julius Caesar," (III, I, 77), *The Complete Works of William Shakespeare*, ed. W.J. Craig (London: Oxford University Press, 1905), 831.

5 Tan, "Judge Chooses to Live Childless," *7,700 Illustrations*, 1197-1198.

6 A. Morgan Derham, "Newton, John (1725-1807)," *The New International Dictionary of the Christian Church*, J.D. Douglas, ed. (Grand Rapid, MI: Zondervan Publishing House, 1974), 704.

7 Ibid., "Booth, William (1829-1912)," 145-146.

8 John V. Dahms, "The Social Interest and Concern of A.B. Simpson," *The Birth of a Vision*, David F. Hartzfeld and Charles Nienkirchen, eds. (Beaverlodge, Alberta: Horizon House Publishers, 1986).

9 Lilly Berry and John Houston, *Psychology at Work* (Madison WI: Brown and Benchmark Publishers, 1993), 82-84.

10 Plutarch, "Morals," cited in John Bartlett, *Familiar Quotations*, 16th ed., Justin Kaplan, ed. (Boston: Little, Brown and Company, 1992), 55:7.

11 Shakespeare, "Hamlet" (I, iii, 77), *Complete Works*, 875.

12 Walt Whitman, "Song of Myself," cited in Bartlett, *Familiar Quotations*, 489:11.

13 Ibid., 489:20.

14 Perhaps an apocryphal line—the myth of the man was larger than life!

15 Tan, "I'm the Greatest," *7,700 Illustrations*, 261.

16 Tan, "Gardener's (Foolish) Prayer," *7,700 Illustrations*, 1044.

8

Ten Promises—The Lord Has a Plan

Zechariah 8:1-23

Again the word of the L*ORD* *Almighty came to me. This is what the* L*ORD* *Almighty says: "I am very jealous for Zion; I am burning with jealousy for her."*

This is what the L*ORD* *says: "I will return to Zion and dwell in Jerusalem. Then Jerusalem will be called the City of Truth, and the mountain of the* L*ORD* *Almighty will be called the Holy Mountain."*

This is what the L*ORD* *Almighty says: "Once again men and women of ripe old age will sit in the streets of Jerusalem, each with cane in hand because of his age. The city streets will be filled with boys and girls playing there."*

This is what the L*ORD* *Almighty says: "It may seem marvelous to the remnant of this people at that time, but will it seem marvelous to me?" declares the* L*ORD* *Almighty.*

This is what the L*ORD* *Almighty says: "I will save my people from the countries of the east and the west. I will bring them back to live in Jerusalem; they will be my people, and I will be faithful and righteous to them as their God."*

This is what the LORD Almighty says: "You who now hear these words spoken by the prophets who were there when the foundation was laid for the house of the LORD Almighty, let your hands be strong so that the temple may be built. Before that time there were no wages for man or beast. No one could go about his business safely because of his enemy, for I had turned every man against his neighbor. But now I will not deal with the remnant of this people as I did in the past," declares the LORD Almighty.

"The seed will grow well, the vine will yield its fruit, the ground will produce its crops, and the heavens will drop their dew. I will give all these things as an inheritance to the remnant of this people. As you have been an object of cursing among the nations, O Judah and Israel, so will I save you, and you will be a blessing. Do not be afraid, but let your hands be strong."

This is what the LORD Almighty says: "Just as I had determined to bring disaster upon you and showed no pity when your fathers angered me," says the LORD Almighty, "so now I have determined to do good again to Jerusalem and Judah. Do not be afraid. These are the things you are to do: Speak the truth to each other, and render true and sound judgment in your courts; do not plot evil against your neighbor, and do not love to swear falsely. I hate all this," declares the LORD.

Again the word of the LORD Almighty came to me. This is what the LORD Almighty says: "The fasts of the fourth, fifth, seventh and tenth months will become joyful and glad occasions and happy festivals for Judah. Therefore love truth and peace."

This is what the LORD Almighty says: "Many peoples and the inhabitants of many cities will yet come, and the inhabitants of one city will go to another and say, 'Let us go at once to entreat the LORD *and seek the* LORD *Almighty. I myself am going.' And many peoples and powerful nations will come to Jerusalem to seek the* LORD *Almighty and to entreat him."*

This is what the LORD *Almighty says: "In those days ten men from all languages and nations will take firm hold of one Jew by the edge of his robe and say, 'Let us go with you, because we have heard that God is with you.'"*

Chapter 7 warned Israel what would happen if they didn't get it right—they would be scattered to the nations. In contrast, chapter 8 draws a picture of God's plan that will include those who *do* get it right, with people from all languages and nations clinging to their coats saying, "Let us go with you, because we have heard that God is with you." This is the way things ought to be! It is the future that God is eager to give.

Chapter 8 concludes the second section of the book. It is the second half of the answer to the question about fasting. But it also prefaces the prophetic future material that follows. It is not a chronological outline, but an outline of main themes presented as a message to God's people, seeking to shape our attitudes as we anticipate what He has planned for us. This chapter expresses the heart of God, describing what He wants to do and what He is waiting to do for His people because of His burning jealousy for them.

Chapters 9-14, the third major section of Zechariah's book, describe events that were all future to Zechariah, some of which are still future today.

People want to know what is in the future. John Walvoord has written numerous books on the subject of prophecy. In 1984 he wrote a book entitled *Armageddon, Oil, and the Middle East Crisis: What the Bible Says about the Future of the Middle East and the End of Western Civilization*. His revised manuscript for a second edition was in the hands of the publisher in 1990 when President Bush sent half a million soldiers to Saudi Arabia. Weeks later, with his book freshly reissued, Dr. Walvoord found himself on morning talk shows and being interviewed by major journalists. Newspapers gave substantial space to report his views. Hundreds of thousands of copies of his book, picturing an American F-15 Eagle fighter plane in the desert, were snapped up.[1] People want to know what the future holds.

Millions expect (and perhaps fear) that the Bible has something to say about that future. They are right, of course. God wants us to know some things about the future and the Bible addresses it extensively.

For the people from Bethel who asked if they could exchange their fasting for feasting (Zechariah 7:2-3), who wanted to know if the promised blessings were about to replace their years of penitent grieving, God's first word was a stiff warning and reorientation (7:4-14). His second word, in chapter 8, was the encouraging plan He had for them. He wanted them to know that He had "determined to do good again to Jerusalem and Judah" (8:15). It was a strong statement. God had decided it, they could expect it to happen!

The title of this chapter is "The Lord Has a Plan." If there had been room for a subtitle, it would have been

"Ten You-Can-Bank-on-It Promises from the Lord." Each promise is preceded by the line, "This is what the LORD Almighty says." The repetition is emphatic. There are many things about the future that we know for sure. Ten are outlined here. Much of what we read in the popular books on the subject is intensely interesting because of the ingenious scenario spinning that goes beyond the hard data. Stories circulate from time to time about the numbered letters of the name of a current statesperson adding up to 666, or some construction on fragments of biblical prophecy that identify the year of the Lord's return. If all of that is exciting at first, it is obvious before long that it is fanciful. So we tire of the speculation because the authors of these schemes are not modest enough to make the distinction between the biblical data and their own vision spinning. But it is a mistake to refuse to consider the future because of that. God has often encouraged His people in stressful times with promises about the future, both general and specific. Let's make sure that we know what He wants us to know.

These ten solid promises about the future are conveniently grouped around four questions that we often ask. "What is in the future?" "When will the blessing begin?" "Does the arrival of blessing require prayer and fasting?" "Who will be saved?"

What Is in The Future? (8:1-8)

First is the "What is going to happen?" question. For Judah it was "Are we done taking the punishment that our grandparents' generation deserved because of their sin? Can we leave the past in the past and start over? We have a building project here. With that new beginning, can we start the new era that the prophets have promised?" They wanted to know if they were done with the hard stuff.

The question for us is exactly the opposite. We live in a culture that has enjoyed religious freedom and prosperity beyond the experience of every previous generation of Christians. We look at the future and wonder with anxiety if our economy is going to crash or if current developments in the Middle East might suddenly lurch us all into something very ominous. The question for us is, "Are we going to lose it?" We press to ask if we are about to move into an age of unprecedented trouble. What is in the future for us? The prophet's answers are in verses 1-8.

They are one-liners. In fact, they are the main themes of previous prophetic messages, developed in detail by Isaiah and others. Some of what we find here is a review of what Zechariah has already said in previous chapters. The Lord reaffirms what they had already heard: 1) "I am very jealous for Zion . . . burning with jealousy" (8:2); 2) "I will return to Zion and dwell in Jerusalem. Then Jerusalem will be called the City of Truth" (8:3); 3) "Once again men and women of ripe old age will sit in the streets of Jerusalem. . . . The city streets will be filled with boys and girls playing there" (8:4-5); 4) "It may seem marvelous to the remnant of this people at that time" (8:6); and 5) "I will save my people from the countries of the east and the west. I will bring them back to live in Jerusalem; they will be my people, and I will be faithful and righteous to them as their God" (8:7-8).

1. *First, we can be sure that God cares very deeply about the strain and the unfairness and the hurt that we live with (8:2).*

For those who may have questioned, "Is God out there? Does He care?," He gave to the prophet a vision of the Angel of the Lord among the myrtle trees, a picture of His presence in the land, receiving messages from all over the world. He knows what is going on. He knows what people suffer. The vision was interpreted by the angel guide with this instruction: "Proclaim this word: This is what the LORD Almighty says: 'I am very jealous for Jerusalem and Zion' " (1:14). "Jealous" seems to be a curious choice of word here because it has negative connotations. It's something we ought not to feel. But in this instance, it certainly means "to be zealous," as some of our translations will have it.[2] God feels our pain very deeply, and we can be sure He will do something about it. He cares for us. That is a secure piece of our future.

2. Second, we can be sure that He will come again to live in Jerusalem (8:3). In the third scene of his vision, Zechariah saw a man preparing to survey the site where the city of Jerusalem once stood. When the prophet asked what was happening, he was told, "The Lord has plans for this place." And then by special delivery this word was brought to him: " 'Jerusalem will be a city without walls because of the great number of men and livestock in it. And I myself will be a wall of fire around it,' declares the LORD, 'and I will be its glory within' " (2:4-5). The rest of chapter 2 is a beautiful piece of Hebrew poetry that begins to tell about what it will be like to have the Lord living there again.

It is really going to happen! The Lord affirms it again in the word before us here. He adds, "Then Jerusalem will be called the City of Truth and . . . the Holy Mountain" (8:3). Jerusalem could hardly be called the City of Truth now. Three major religions claim it as a holy place. Jewish people do because it was David's capital and the site of their temple. Christians do because Jesus was crucified and resurrected there. Muslims do because it is the place from which Mohammed was taken to heaven by the angel Gabriel, they say, to speak with God. Every one of these major religions claims to represent the truth. And each is represented in the city by many subjects, all vying for recognition as the guardians of the truth. Jerusalem is not the City of Truth—it is the city of confusion. Where one might expect to enjoy the quiet contemplation of truth, like in the Church of the Holy Sepulcher or on the Mount of Olives, truth is obscured by thousands of curious tourists, and devotion is robbed by the boy with the olive wood trinkets pressing to relieve you of your change.

If it is not yet the City of Truth, can it be considered the Holy Mountain? The first time that my wife Joan and I were in Israel, our tour guide was proud to tell us that he was a native-born Israeli. From the airport, we proceeded directly to Jerusalem, approaching the city as the sun was going down. Along the way, our wonderfully warm and entertaining leader began to extol the city. In his broken English, he talked about Jerusalem as the holy place, the high place, the revered place of all the nations, very special to Jewish people. He told us that our bus driver named Yitsak was born in Jerusalem. "I am special among the Jews—I was born in Israel. Yitsak was born in Jerusalem. He is special among the special," he explained.

The next morning we were taken to the top of the Mount of Olives where we saw stretched out before us the Kidron Valley and the Old City, so familiar from the many photographs we'd seen. What a moment! What a feeling! This was the Holy City!

It did not take us long to recognize the pious and commercial hype. Jerusalem is full of religious apparatus, but godlessness permeates. There is not much there that reinforces any preconceived sense of holiness. If you did not bring it with you, you are not apt to find it in the tension and busyness of the city itself. In spite of the efforts of the Israeli government to lure you there with Holy City promotion, it really is not a holy city.

But when Jesus returns, He will establish Himself in Jerusalem, and He will personally establish truth and holiness there as dominant characteristics of the city He has chosen.

3. *Third, we can be sure that it will be a time of peace, a time of perfect security for both old and young (8:4-5).* It is hard for us to imagine peace in the Middle East. We want to hope that peace initiatives will succeed, but the obstacles are formidable.

Our first impressions of Israel began with the security arrangements in Ben Gurion Airport. Eighteen-year-old Israelis with machine guns patrol security checkpoints. And they are tense. It took me a while to decide to relax and to conclude that with that protection we were as safe there as anywhere in the world. But it is obvious that Jerusalem is not a city of peace. Soldiers perch on the gates of the Old City periodically checking handbags as people enter. Sipping cappuccino on a Saturday night on Ben Yehuda Street in modern West Jerusalem, enjoying the carnival atmosphere at the end of the Sabbath, somehow it was hard to relax. I was distracted by the foot patrols of young soldiers, both men and women, in pairs or small groups, coming by often and checking for suspicious packages in garbage cans.

On the Lebanon border, as we stood at a military installation and looked across a solemn razor wire fence that made us shudder, I debated the propriety of taking a picture, fearful of offending our well-armed hosts. Marlis, a young woman traveling with us, abruptly and fearlessly approached a group of about twenty young Israeli soldiers and said, "I want to have my picture taken with you." One took the clip out of an automatic rifle and gave her the gun to hold while they all posed for us. In a treasured picture, her blond hair and bright casual tourist clothing stand out in striking contrast to their dark Mediterranean features and combat fatigues—a lamb among lions. It reminds me of the contrast of the Lord's promise of peace for Jerusalem against the backdrop of what we see there now.

Isaiah's prophetic vision of Jerusalem was of a city where swords will be recast as plowshares. He said there will come a day when all of that military apparatus over there that demands first priority on their strained economic resources will be turned into farm implements. The equipment of war will no longer be necessary. The Lord told Isaiah:

> Behold, I will create new heavens and a new earth. The former things will not be remembered, nor will they come to mind. . . . Never again will there be in it an infant who lives but a few days, or an old man who does not live out

> his years; he who dies at a hundred will be thought a mere youth; he who fails to reach a hundred will be considered accursed. (Isaiah 65:17, 20)

Zechariah can envision people relaxing on Ben Yehuda Street without the possibility of a terrorist attack, surrounded by carefree children whose mothers will no longer need to rake the school's sandboxes early each morning for fear of button bombs. It will be so completely different; it will be a new heaven and a new earth. A world without war. A time of peace.

4. *Next, we can be sure that what the Lord does will seem marvelous to those who experience it (8:6).* The Hebrew word for "marvelous" is translated differently in Isaiah 9:6. We have put the verse to music and warmly sing, "His name is *Wonderful*." Our experience of the Lord's love is very special to us. "He's the Great Shepherd, the Rock of all Ages, Almighty God is He." It is clear that His strong love and His return and His reign of peace will be marvelous to us too—a wonderful experience.

But more than the warmth of our experience is indicated here. Perhaps we need to hyphenate the word to get the point. The Lord is "wonderful," but now consider that He is "wonder-full." He is always doing things that are miraculous. After these first descriptions of future developments, He asks us to consider, "Does this seem hard to believe? It may be incredible to you, but not to Me." What seems to us to be miraculous or marvelous will be normal! A miracle is an abnormal development that breaks into the cause-and-effect of natural sequence, but those things are normal to the Lord. So expect that when He comes to live among His people again, the miracles that are so much a part of the stories of Jesus in the Gospels will again be common occurrences.

Doesn't it seem that it would take a miracle to undo the ecological disaster that our world has become? The Lord simply says that He plans to renew the earth.

We elect a president with a mandate to restore our prosperity, take care of our national deficit, give us more government services and ensure our national and social security—all of this, of course, with reduced taxes. Who can possibly do this? The man cannot give us the millennium. We should not be disappointed when he is unable to give us the miracles we ask for. But when Jesus comes He will reign over an age of remarkable (and secure) prosperity.

We want a justice system that is simple and fair. The Lord promises to come and reign Himself in righteousness. We want a world that is not full of the hatred and killing and war that dominate our news every night. It seems that we in the U.S. just got over Nicaragua in time to get into Kuwait; the euphoria of winning the Gulf War was soon lost in the apparently insolubility of Bosnia and the volatility of Korea; our good intentions in Somalia got caught in the crossfire of local ancient feuds, and we didn't even want to talk about Rwanda; the euphoria of communism's collapse slid into the chaos of the ungovernability of Russia. But the Lord simply says that He plans to bring peace, and though it will seem utterly marvelous to us, from His perspective it is not even a stretch.

Then we bring to this the injustices that have violated us, the impossibilities that wear us down and the mountains that will not move in our homes, in our work and sometimes deep inside ourselves. The Lord says firmly that what seems impossible for us is normal for Him. And when He comes again, all of those things will be taken care of.

5. *We can also be sure that the Jewish people will come from the east and the west (8:7-8).* It is one of the wonders of the last 100 years. Very difficult developments in central and eastern Europe have produced an intermittent stream of Jewish refugees ready to find refuge in Israel and to build a new nation. With that, Jews whose families had lived for generations in other countries in the Middle East and North Africa found living there to be increasingly intolerable, so they came too. They continue to come, as world spasms make them victims. But they come mostly from the lands of the East.

Here God says that they will come from both east and west. To date, very few of the Jews in the United States and the West have gone to Israel. Life is comfortable here, and they have become prosperous. But before the fulfillment of this prophecy is complete, it seems that they will emigrate from the West too, which leaves dangling the question of what developments might prompt that!

And the Jews will once again be His people. Spiritual revival will be added to the national revival. As much as anything else outlined here, that would certainly be wonder-full. Many modern Jews have left behind the God of their tradition in their pursuit of prosperity. Their Jewishness is more heritage than religion. Others are pious, fanatically sectarian, rigidly defending their religious regimens and their superior and singular righteousness. Where in all of this is there a warm sense of a faithful and righteous God? But the promise stands out in bold relief against current realities. You can be sure that the Jewish people will return to the land, and you can be sure that they will again be the devout people of God.

What is in the future for us? Dramatic change. The answers here are augmented by this scenario in the New Testament:

> And I saw an angel coming down out of heaven, having the key to the Abyss and holding in his hand a great chain. He seized the dragon, that ancient serpent, who is the devil, or Satan, and bound him for a thousand years. He threw him into the Abyss, and locked and sealed it over him, to keep him from deceiving the nations anymore. . . .
>
> I saw thrones on which were seated those who had been given authority to judge. And I saw the souls of those who had been beheaded because of their testimony for Jesus and because of the word of God. They had not worshiped the beast or his image and had not received his mark on their foreheads or their hands. They came to life and reigned with Christ a thousand years. (The rest of the dead did not come to life until the thousand years were ended.) This is the first resurrection. Blessed and holy are those who have part in the first resurrection. The second death has no power over them, but they

> will be priests of God and of Christ and will reign with him for a thousand years. (Revelation 20:1-6)

The Lord repeatedly says that He intends to come to earth to reign.

What is going to happen? It is important to get these pieces firmly in place. God wants us to recognize that the first answer to the question is that He knows when we suffer, and the second answer is that in the end He will draw together all of His people in a renewed world where He will reign personally. Those two certainties bracket everything else that may happen between now and then. With this perspective, it all seems more manageable, for though it is marvelous to us, it is not marvelous to God.

When Does the Blessing Begin? (8:9-17)

It seems that whenever I preach on the subject of future things, it doesn't matter how fully I develop the text somebody will ask the "when?" question. Clearly it is a hot button, touching a deep anxiety. We are most anxious about the prophesied increase in troubles that will convulse the world. And in our fear we want to know when! Our insecurity presses forward the wrong question. It is much more important to ask "what?" and "who?" Unfortunately, our sense that it could well be soon is exploited by speakers and writers who come very close to telling us exactly what we insist we want to know. If the failure of a succession of their predictions does not turn us sour against prophecy altogether, Jesus' warning about date predictors should give us the discernment to know when to turn off the radio or throw away the book (see Mark 13:32). Nobody knows when.

But there is an answer to the "when" question that is very satisfying if we are prepared to accept something other than date-fixing and to be content with what the Lord wants to tell us. First, we need to ask the question more precisely. For the delegation from Bethel, it was, "Is the blessing about to begin now? Is it time to 'forget the former things,' as Isaiah said, and 'not dwell on the past' (Isaiah 43:18-21), as we have done in our strictly observed fasts? With our new temple, is the great age of blessing about to begin?" There will not be satisfying answers if we try to predict the rapture or the emergence of the Antichrist. But there are two good answers here to the question of when to expect the promised blessing.

6. *The first answer to the question, and the sixth affirmation in the series, is given in Zechariah 8:9-11:*

> This is what the LORD Almighty says: "You who now hear these words spoken by the prophets who were there when the foundation was laid for the house of the LORD Almighty, . . . let your hands be strong so that the temple may be built. Before that time there were no wages for man or beast. No one could go about his business safely because of his enemy, for I had turned every man against his neighbor. But *now* I will not deal with the remnant of this people as I did in the past," declares the LORD Almighty. (emphasis added)

Haggai reminded them that their farming would be

blessed and that, instead of being an object of cursing among the nations, they would be a blessing to their neighbors. Zechariah's answer in recalling the prophetic word at the resumption of the building project was simply this: "The blessing has already begun." In fact, he says, "It began on December 18, 520 B.C., two years ago" (see Haggai 2:15-19).

Haggai had a graphic, forceful message earlier that year for the folks who were experiencing financial trouble:

> Now this is what the LORD Almighty says: "Give careful thought to your ways. You have planted much, but have harvested little. You eat, but never have enough. You drink, but never have your fill. You put on clothes, but are not warm. You earn wages, only to put them in a purse with holes in it."
>
> This is what the LORD Almighty says: "Give careful thought to your ways. Go up into the mountains and bring down timber and build the house, so that I may take pleasure in it and be honored," says the LORD. "You expected much, but see, it turned out to be little. What you brought home, I blew away. Why?" declares the LORD Almighty. "Because of my house, which remains a ruin, while each of you is busy with his own house. Therefore, because of you the heavens have withheld their dew and the earth its crops. I called for a drought on the fields and the mountains, on the grain, the new wine, the oil and whatever the ground produces, on men and cattle, and on the labor of your hands." (1:5-11)

What he was saying to them was, "What are you waiting for? You will never be able to afford what God is asking you to do. Is He asking you to build a new building? Don't wait for Him to fill you with His blessing before you begin. Your obedience must come first. Don't wait until you have enough money in the bank. You will never have it! Your purse has a hole in it. Don't wait until you think you can afford it to begin doing work on the temple." They got the point. Within days they began work. A few months later, it was time to lay the cornerstone. With that substantial start, at the ceremony to set the stone, the prophet brought another word from the Lord for the occasion.

> "Now give careful thought to this from this day on—consider how things were before one stone was laid on another in the LORD's temple. When anyone came to a heap of twenty measures, there were only ten. When anyone went to a wine vat to draw fifty measures, there were only twenty. I struck all the work of your hands with blight, mildew and hail, yet you did not turn to me,' declares the LORD. [But then,] From this day on, from this twenty-fourth day of the ninth month, give careful thought to the day when the foundation of the LORD's temple was laid. . . .
>
> "From this day on I will bless you." (2:15-19)

There was significant, tangible blessing that came with their obedience—the hand of the Lord began to make their circumstances good again. The blessing begins when we step out to do what God commands us to do. Some of that future age of blessing that God has so emphatically promised is in our lives already when we walk in obedience. The first answer to the "when?" question is "already."

The message of Joel three centuries earlier was similar. It was during another time of serious adversity, with wave upon wave of locusts feasting until there was nothing green left in the land. Facing the prospect of starvation, the people heard the prophet call them back to the Lord. The promise He held out to them turns on this familiar line, "*Then* the LORD will be jealous for his land and take pity on his people" (Joel 2:18, emphasis added). In response to their repentance and turning back to the Lord, they would find His heart of blessing had turned back to them. The succession of promises is rich: "I am sending you grain, new wine and oil, enough to satisfy you fully. . . . I will repay you for the years the locusts have eaten. . . .You will have plenty to eat, until you are full, and you will praise the name of the LORD your God" (2:19, 25-26). God feels strongly about human disaster. He wants to give good gifts. "*And afterward*, I will pour out my Spirit on all people. Your sons and your daughters will prophesy, your old men will dream dreams, your young men will see visions. Even on my servants, both men and women, I will pour out my Spirit in those days" (2:28-29, emphasis added). There is a "then" section to this prophecy, and an "afterward" section. The "then" promises, the prophet said, were available as soon as the people returned to God with all their hearts.

When Peter stood up to speak to the Pentecost crowd to explain the wind, the flames of fire on their heads (so much like the Shekinah that once dwelt in the Holy Place) and their miraculous ability to speak in different languages, he said, "This is the 'afterward' that Joel talked about. Some of the blessing of the future has come to us now" (see Acts 2:16-21). The second time the apostles were summoned to the Sanhedrin and told to stop teaching about Jesus, their response to them was,

> We must obey God rather than men! . . . God exalted [Jesus] to his own right hand as Prince and Savior that he might give repentance and forgiveness of sins to Israel. We are witnesses of these things, and so is the Holy Spirit, *whom God has given to those who obey him*. (5:29, 31-32, emphasis added)

Again, the first answer to the "when" question is "already," and it is linked to obedience.

In both Testaments, then, obedience and grace are conjoined. Contrary to the simplistic notion that they are separated by the division of Testaments, we should hear Moses with vivid memories and scorching words remind God's people that they are stiff-necked, chosen by the Lord from among all the nations to be those on whom He would set His affection, not because they were greater than all the other peoples, but simply because He loved them and because He had made a promise to their forefathers (Deuteronomy 7:7-8). That is grace. We should also hear Jesus' last words, directing the eleven to baptize disciples in all nations and to teach them to *obey* everything he had commanded them (Matthew 28:16-20). That is a life of obedience. Our salvation is not earned by obedience, but when it is graciously presented to us, we must be obedient to the message from God about ourselves and about His Son by humbling ourselves as sinners before Him, seeking His mercy and giving our lives in His service.

The blessings stored up for us in the future are not the credits we place on deposit there by righteous living, but rather they are the gracious gifts of the Lord Almighty who burns with a jealous love for His people. Yet our experience of the power of the Spirit in our lives and circumstances, a taste of the blessing that will roll without restriction in the age to come, is clearly linked in both Old and New Testaments to our deliberate decision to walk in obedience. For them the blessing began on the day they laid the cornerstone of the building. For us it begins when we decisively abandon our homemade spirituality and deliberately orient our lives around what God says we should do.

7. *The first part of the answer to the "when" question is that the blessing begins already. The second part of the answer begins in Zechariah 8:14-15.* "This is what the LORD Almighty says: 'Just as I had determined to bring disaster upon you and showed no pity when your fathers angered me,' says the LORD Almighty, 'so now I have determined to do good again to Jerusalem and Judah. Do not be afraid.' "

Consider the line, "I have determined to do good." Simply put, some things are determined by God. He reminded them that there came a point when He determined that His people were going to be sold to the Babylonians. Jeremiah clearly told them that they had crossed the line. Nothing could save them. What had long been a threat, a warning against their sin-saturated life choices, was going to happen (see Jeremiah 11:14-17). Jeremiah was not a popular preacher! Now Zechariah's message is that, just as God once determined "to bring disaster" without pity, He later determined that there will come a time when everything will run the other direction and He will "do good again to Jerusalem and Judah." He had determined destruction, and it happened as He said it would. He has determined blessing, and that will happen as certainly as the destruction. Just as surely as a merciless crushing was their past history, an almost unimaginable blessing would be their future (and ours). So when will the age of blessing begin? It will happen when God determines it will happen!

Knowing who will make it happen is more important for our sense of confidence about the future than knowing when it will happen. It is clear that the Lord is not just considering the possibility. He is not waiting to see if His people will ever get their lives together as if the coming of the age of blessing were hinged on their doing all of the right things good enough or as if it waited for more fervent prayers. He is not waiting for justice and godliness to prevail so that He can then come with His blessing. The fact of the matter is that He has already determined to do this, and what He has determined is future history, a history that is already written. He has set the time. Jesus said that the Father has a fixed "when" (Acts 1:7).

If that makes it seem like living right is a matter of indifference, consider this extension of the thought: "'These are the things you are to do: Speak the truth to each other, and render true and sound judgment in your courts; do not plot evil against your neighbor, and do not love to swear falsely. I hate all this,' declares the LORD" (Zechariah 8:16-17).

Having just been told that the Lord is the One who turned the big switch that directed national disaster, and that He is the One who has fixed the time of the age of gold that is sure to come, it seems appropriate that we should be reminded here how prudent it is to learn what He hates and what pleases Him. The broad strokes of the future are fixed by God's authority. The shorter strokes, our personal experiences of destruction or blessing, are the result of a mix of developments and decisions, the Lord's intervention in our history and our responses to these things. The same holy God, so dramatically presented many times in this chapter as "The LORD Almighty," controls the little switches of destruction and blessing as well. Perhaps it is time to recover a real sense of the "fear of the Lord."

The simple lesson in these two verses gets to the heart of the matter. The prophet promotes learning to do what pleases the Lord and turning from the things He hates.

When does the blessing begin? First of all, the outpouring of blessing has already begun. So we are prodded by the prophet to walk in obedient service and to expect that God will protect us and prosper us and give us peace (8:9-13). And secondly, the age of blessing will roll when God says it is time to roll, and that will be a tremendous reverse in the flow of history. We ought to live our lives in humble recognition of his power to determine what happens next (8:14-17).

Does the Arrival of Blessing Require Prayer and Fasting? (8:18-19)

The third question this message from the Lord answers is in fact the first one that the people asked. Should we seek the blessing by prayer and fasting? Or, as the delegation from Bethel asked it, "Can we stop fasting now and get on with the blessing?" (see Zechariah 7:3). Many Jewish people of our generation are seeking to do that as well.

In Israel today, what was called for centuries the "Wailing Wall" is now known as the "Western Wall." It is the only piece left of the second temple that was being built at the time of Zechariah. For years Jews have gone to the wall to pour out their tears because of the loss of their temple and their city. Written prayers on little papers are wedged into the stones of all that remains of the great temple. During some periods of history, Jews were not allowed into the city, so they would camp on the hills around Jerusalem and cry out to the Lord there in sight of the wall on their great days of national mourning. Within hours after the Jewish troops took the Old City of Jerusalem in the first week of June 1967, the Arab shanty town that had stood before the wall was demolished to make a large open square, and thousands of Jews thronged in. They no longer call it the "Wailing Wall" because with this stunning turn in history they had their city back. Similarly, in the story before us, they were coming up to the day when they would have their temple back. Did they still need to be wailing?

Some modern Jews are determined that the Holocaust must never be forgotten. Joan and I have visited the Yad VaShem Museum, the Holocaust memorial in Jerusalem. The pictures and the descriptions are graphic. A piece of film made by the Nazis shows several dozen naked, shockingly emaciated people before a freshly prepared ditch. It is stunning to watch a spray of machine gunfire shooting them all with a force that threw them into the trench. The bulldozers were already running, prepared to bury them there. Some of those who survived the death camps of Europe, including many whose number tattoos on their arms are badges of their horror, are determined that the memory of it should unite us all in determination that nothing like that should ever be permitted to happen again. They do not want the world to forget. They do not want their children to forget. But some of their children would like to put that national nightmare behind them and not have it dominate their lives. Like them, Zechariah's audience was a new generation of Jews asking if they could be released from the burden of their parents' memories. The blessing was beginning. Their hostile neighbors were held at bay by the edict of the emperor. The temple project was underway. What about the fasting?

We ask a different question about fasting. Why fast? It seems extreme, medieval, ascetic. We much prefer to "live like king's kids." Occasionally someone with great spiritual ardor will stand up and remind us that every revival we have ever known has been preceded by fervent prayer. Sometimes there is a chiding implication in it, if not a direct challenge, that if we do not have revival it is because of our failure to pray, or to pray enough, or perhaps our failure to pray and fast with the right intensity.

8. *The answer to the question is in verse 19: "This is what the LORD Almighty says: 'The fasts of the fourth, fifth, seventh and tenth months will become joyful and glad occasions and happy festivals for Judah. Therefore love truth and peace.' "* That is to say, there will come a time when you will not need to fast anymore. Be content with that short answer. Your reward will not be when you finally figure out how to do your fasting right. Instead, anticipate the time when fasts will all become feasts, not by doing your spiritual exercises more fastidiously, but by living right. The prophetic message again comes back to truth and peace.

The Pharisees had this wrong, and so do some of us. They were masters of the traditional spiritual exercises. They interrupted with a word of rebuke when they saw the careless breaking of the rule—Jesus' disciples snacking on wheat kernels on a day of fasting, for example. Clearly He had not taught them the appropriate disciplines of spirituality! Jesus brushed aside their objection and even answered the concerns of John's ascetic disciples by telling them a time would come when His disciples would fast—after He had left them (Matthew 9:14-15; Mark 2:18-20). He sought to shift the emphasis to more important matters like truth and peace.

We live in a broken world. Fasting is still appropriate. We mourn the evil and hurt around us, and we mourn how we and people we love have been caught in it. Fasting can be an intensified form of prayer. Sometimes spiritual forces are only defeated by prayer and fasting, as Jesus Himself taught (Mark 9:28-29). Or we fast for discipline, making our bodies our slaves as the apostle Paul said, being sure that our physical instincts are under control (1 Corinthians 9:27). Sometimes we simply fast for our health. But fasting and spiritual routines should never be construed as leverage that will make God give us what we are demanding of Him—even if it is revival.

But if it is correct to say that we live in a time when fasting is entirely appropriate, it is also right to say that we live in a time when feasting is appropriate. We mourn current realities, some of which have us caught in their web. Yet we celebrate future realities, some of which have reached back to include us in them already. Someday the hurt, stress, confusion, failure, loss, disappointment and fear that are a normal part of life will all be over. All of our grieving, mourning and fasting will be replaced by celebration. This is what the Lord Almighty says. Do not forget the past, but keep your eye on the future.

And love truth and peace. We are confident that God has acted in history and we fully expect Him to do so again, turning all of our fasts into festivals. We are not unrealistic about the world's horrors so that we live in a naive and self-deluded world. Nor are we morose and negative, ignorant of the Lord's gift of a profound future that He is even now preparing for His people. Instead, we are free to leave with Him our past and our future and to patiently follow the way that He has laid out for us to walk. His promise of a festival future helps us keep our balance in a fasting and celebrating time until then.

Who Will Be Saved? (8:20-23)

Who would be included in the blessing? Those returned from exile seemed so few. There were not enough of them to begin to renew their once magnificent capital city. Could it be possible that the God of all the world and of all of history would do all of this for them, a small remnant of a once great nation? And what about all the others? Were they all going to be lost out there somewhere? For us the question is similar: Will God really destroy those who do not believe (especially some we love)? The issue is distressing for many.

The chapters that follow Zechariah 8 tell us that many will lose their lives in the catastrophes ahead. Those who resist the Lord will find themselves on the wrong side of the great conflict to come. Those who survive will come to Jerusalem to pay homage to the King, the Lord Almighty, where He will reign over a renewed creation. But in the end, it will not be just such a pitiful few who will come into the great blessing God has planned.

9. This is what the LORD Almighty says: "Many peoples and the inhabitants of many cities will yet come, and the inhabitants of one city will go to another and say, 'Let us go at once to entreat the LORD and seek the LORD Almighty. I myself am going.' And many peoples and powerful nations will come to Jerusalem to seek the LORD Almighty and to entreat him." (8:20-22)

When "the LORD moved the heart of Cyrus" to release the Jews from their exile and to encourage them to rebuild the temple at Jerusalem, 42,360 people—"everyone whose heart God had moved"—volunteered to return (Ezra 1:1, 5). It all happened so fast but the momentum had not been sustained. Several provincial towns had been reestablished, but even years later Nehemiah found that there were few who actually lived in Jerusalem (Nehemiah 7:4). Most of the Jews had settled into life in Babylon or Egypt. Most of those who had come back to the land were more or less comfortable in their rural communities, close to the land. It seemed that nobody wanted to tackle the challenges of rebuilding the city. The prophetic word about Jerusalem being the center of God's plan to bless His people would stretch their imaginations to the limit.

Among all of the other good things that the Lord has determined to do is move people from many communities to Jerusalem. When the Lord is established in residence there, it will be *the* place to be. Will there only be a remnant to enjoy the blessing? Quite clearly no! The Lord will draw folks from all over to come to Him in that very place.

10. This is what the LORD Almighty says: "In those days ten men from all languages and nations will take firm hold of one Jew by the hem of his robe and say, 'Let us go with you, because we have heard that God is with you.' " (Zechariah 8:23)

If it was not clear in the previous verses that this will be an international movement, that is the emphasis in this one. The promises are for more than the miserable remnant. They are for "men from all languages and nations." The scope of God's plan is much greater than what the temple-building crew would be inclined to think, extending far beyond the Jewish people.

The message is clear: Those who "did not listen" (7:13), even those among the people of God, are scattered with a whirlwind. Those who come to "entreat the LORD" (8:21-22) will find Him, irrespective of their nationality. The promise is of a great gathering of people hungry for God. More than that, it is a picture of the Lord resident among the Jewish people in their capital city, attracting others from many language groups and nations to Him there.

Joel was another prophet who brought a dual message of judgment and blessing. With him, the conclusion was an exhortation to choose which side of this great divide you would be on because "the day of the LORD is near in the valley of decision" (Joel 3:14). He foresaw:

> wonders in the heavens
> and on the earth,
> blood and fire and billows of smoke.
> The sun will be turned to darkness
> and the moon to blood
> before the coming of the great and dreadful
> day of the LORD.
> And everyone who calls
> on the name of the LORD will be saved;
> for on Mount Zion and in Jerusalem
> there will be deliverance,
> as the LORD has said,
> among the survivors
> whom the LORD calls. (2:30-32)

The deliverance He promised will be for those who come to Him to be saved, so that in that day of terrible judgment, "the LORD will be a refuge for his people" (3:16). So the survivors will be called to the Lord when He sets up His throne in Jerusalem.

Peter drew on this prophetic word to urge the Pentecost crowd to seek God before the Day of the

Lord arrives (Acts 2:19-21). The prophet Hosea said, "It is time to seek the LORD, until he comes and showers righteousness on you" (Hosea 10:12). The battle lines are forming and the movement has begun. Men and women and young people from every nation are already coming to Him, an international ingathering anticipating the literal scenes of the prophetic word before us. The components of the picture are being assembled. Zechariah's answer to their fasting question draws alternative conclusions, and implicitly insists on a choice. We can inherit the whirlwind of chapter 7 or we can inherit the determined blessing of chapter 8. In the end, "everyone who calls on the name of the Lord will be saved" (Joel 2:32; Acts 2:21; Romans 10:13). And in the end, those coming to Him from the nations will outnumber the Jews.

These promises about the future ought to give a sense of large and permanent value to the work we do for the Lord: "Let your hands be strong so that the temple may be built" (Zechariah 8:9). These promises ought to fortify our faulty faith: "Do not be afraid" (8:15). They ought to shape our sense of morality: " 'Speak the truth . . . render true and sound judgment . . . do not plot evil . . . do not love to swear falsely. I hate all this,' declares the LORD" (8:16-17). They ought to add happy festivals to our seasons of fasting as we anticipate the future, seeking truth and peace (8:19). And there ought to resonate in our hearts this word of the Lord's fixed intention: "So now I have determined to do good again to Jerusalem and Judah" (8:15). That is the way things ought to be.

Discussion Questions for Further Study

1. What about the future makes you anxious?
2. What difference would it make in our world if Jesus were resident here?
3. What are some of the "mountains that don't move" in your life or in our world? Which should you challenge (Matthew 17:20), and which should you leave for the Lord to look after in His time (2 Corinthians 12:7-9)?
4. What are some of the blessings that will roll when the Lord returns that we can begin to enjoy already?
5. Which, if any, of the commandments in Zechariah 8:16-17 strike you as something you should obey more carefully?
6. On what occasions should we be fasting and penitent? What occasions should be times of feasting and celebration?
7. If the Lord gives your neighbors a heart to seek Him and His blessing, what is there about your life that would make them want to come to you and ask you to take them with you to meet the Lord? Are there changes you need to make to become more attractive in this way?
8. Which of the ten promises in this chapter is the most important one for you to hold on to? Why?

Endnotes

[1] John F. Walvoord, *Armageddon, Oil and the Middle East Crisis: What the Bible Says about the Future of the Middle East and the End of Western Civilization*, rev. ed. (Grand Rapids: Zondervan Publishing House, 1990).

[2] New King James Version.

Part 3

The Way Things Will Be

9

Learning to Live with the Promise

Zechariah 9:1-10:1

An Oracle

The word of the LORD is against the land of
Hadrach
and will rest upon Damascus—
for the eyes of men and all the tribes of Israel
are on the LORD—
and upon Hamath too, which borders on it,
and upon Tyre and Sidon, though they are
very skillful.
Tyre has built herself a stronghold;
she has heaped up silver like dust,
and gold like the dirt of the streets.
But the Lord will take away her possessions
and destroy her power on the sea,
and she will be consumed by fire.
Ashkelon will see it and fear;
Gaza will writhe in agony,
and Ekron too, for her hope will wither.
Gaza will lose her king
and Ashkelon will be deserted.

Foreigners will occupy Ashdod,
and I will cut off the pride of the Philistines.
I will take the blood from their mouths,
the forbidden food from between their teeth.
Those who are left will belong to our God
and become leaders in Judah,
and Ekron will be like the Jebusites.
But I will defend my house
against marauding forces.
Never again will an oppressor overrun my people,
for now I am keeping watch.

Rejoice greatly, O Daughter of Zion!
Shout, Daughter of Jerusalem!
See, your king comes to you,
righteous and having salvation,
gentle and riding on a donkey,
on a colt, the foal of a donkey.
I will take away the chariots from Ephraim
and the war-horses from Jerusalem,
and the battle bow will be broken.
He will proclaim peace to the nations.
His rule will extend from sea to sea
and from the River to the ends of the earth.
As for you, because of the blood of my covenant with you,
I will free your prisoners from the waterless pit.
Return to your fortress, O prisoners of hope;
even now I announce that I will restore twice as much to you.
I will bend Judah as I bend my bow

and fill it with Ephraim.
I will rouse your sons, O Zion,
against your sons, O Greece,
and make you like a warrior's sword.

Then the Lord will appear over them;
his arrow will flash like lightning.
The Sovereign Lord will sound the trumpet;
he will march in the storms of the south,
and the Lord Almighty will shield them.
They will destroy
and overcome with slingstones.
They will drink and roar as with wine;
they will be full like a bowl
used for sprinkling the corners of the altar.
The Lord their God will save them on that day
as the flock of his people.
They will sparkle in his land
like jewels in a crown.
How attractive and beautiful they will be!
Grain will make the young men thrive,
and new wine the young women.

Ask the Lord for rain in the springtime;
it is the Lord who makes the storm clouds.
He gives showers of rain to men,
and plants of the field to everyone.

As we come to the last chapters of the book of Zechariah, a word of orientation is in order. There is a natural break between chapters 8 and 9. Some think that what follows may have been written forty years later than the previous material.[1] That may be the case.

What we find here has no specific reference of occasion or original context. It seems detached from current realities, a peering into the future.

We can splice together some fragments of background data, however, that may help us understand why these oracles were given to Zechariah's congregation in the later years of his life. With the encouragement of Haggai and Zechariah and prophetic messages from the Lord, the people worked together to finish the construction of the second temple. It wasn't much compared to the one that Solomon had built which had been destroyed seventy years earlier. But it was an uplifting start to the rebuilding of Jerusalem. Years later, the momentum that had raised the building drained off into a plodding do-the-best-you-can-with-what-you-have-and-cut-the-corners-where-you-must existence. The blessings that the prophets promised had not materialized. The people had a taste of that blessing in the building process but as the years went by the spiritual landscape slid into a depressing state. These chapters were given to people who were not very buoyant spiritually. They needed this vision of the future and the gripping sense throughout these messages of the One who is in charge. So do we.

We find two oracles here. The first is in chapters 9-11, the second is in chapters 12-14. An oracle is a word from the Lord, not in the form of a prophetic sermon or lively Hebrew poetry, like much of the writings of the prophets, but more literally a word-for-word message. In a special sense, these are God's words, and He comes to say, "Let Me tell you what is going to happen in the future." These are especially hopeful when life seems cyclical, when this year is not any different from last year, when tomorrow has little possibility of being an improvement on today.

So these messages are for us too. They are for people who are only aiming to survive, whose bumper stickers say, "Life is hard and then you die," or "He who has the most toys in the end wins." It is for the one who lives with a sense that his or her life is futile and not going anywhere. There is a clear message here that history is not randomly unfolding, that God is an active force in how it develops and that He is taking it in a specific direction. With these oracles He is going to show us where.

This is also a hopeful message when we *do* have a sense that our history is going somewhere and we are very uncomfortable about where it seems to be taking us. Not many people are genuinely hopeful about the future. With what the Lord reveals to us, we have reason to be both pessimistic and optimistic concerning what is to come, as we will see with the unfolding of these chapters. What we are shown here gives us information about what we will find along the way to a dramatic and wonderful conclusion, with a realistic sense of both the fact of evil and the sovereignty of God.

Brad Stevenson is the pastor of Resurrection Alliance Church in Bowling Green, Kentucky. With that identity, it was poignant when he spoke in our church one Sunday night and he asked us to encourage each other with "evidences of the resurrection." We used to call that "testimony time," or more recently we have overused the weaker term "sharing." There was a buoyancy in Brad's fresh approach, and of course we could find daily indicators in our lives that the Lord is alive and that He loves us still. It is interesting to me that when we do that (whatever we may call it), we tend to measure evidence of the resurrection in little developments—small needs that the Lord notices and stories of His tender care. So we talk about the "mercy drops" falling around us—and we should! We really ought to be grateful for each one.

Another guest in our church a while back was John Walvoord, a lifetime student of prophecy and the author of many books on the subject. He always seeks to sense the great sweep of what God is doing. When we shared breakfast together, Dr. Walvoord teased his wife about noticing the little things. He said that she is the kind who always prays that God will provide a parking spot right in front of the building where she wants to go. And he laughed as he confessed, "She gets more parking places than I do!" Then in genuine self-deprecation, he observed that he may miss noticing some of God's little graces because his focus has always been on the horizon, looking for the larger developments brought about by the hand of God.

It is delightful to recognize God's hand in the little circumstances of our lives. But it is equally important to understand that He moves in dramatic ways, and we ought to be expectantly watching for such instances. The daily news is not likely to tie major developments to the hand of God. But these prophecies in the last section of Zechariah will help us to track the movements of God on the larger screen. It is my judgment that in our lifetime we will see some of these things happen, and we need to recognize them for what they are.

The oracles of Zechariah are an invitation to look for the big movements of God. Thank God for the mercy drops, but be reminded that He is capable of "showers of blessing" too. Our minds and hearts are expanded as we learn to live with the promise. We are the "prisoners of hope" in 9:12. Though we are bound by the realities of a broken world and live with our own brokenness, we can still be hopeful. These chapters set out to give the gift of hope.

One more word of orientation as we get into the text: The Hebrew people thought thematically; we tend to think chronologically. It is important to read these oracles for what they say, looking for the themes, not for the time lines. There are "not yet" periods between dramatic developments, so we must not lose sight of the promise of the Lord when everything seems to be stalled and when in our impatience it appears that He is not doing much. Then when developments really are stormy, we must not lose sight of the Lord in the action or be overwhelmed by the turbulence.

Chapter 9 will help us learn to live with the promise. We will find here the Promise of Protection (9:1-8), the Promise of Salvation (9:9-10) and the Promise of Release (9:11-10:1).

The Promise of Protection (9:1-8)

There is another aspect of the word "oracle." Besides being a word-for-word message, it also bears a sense that it is heavy, a burden to deliver. The issues at hand are grave. The first eight verses can be summarized by the warning in verse 1, "The word of the LORD is against the land of Hadrach," and the promise in verse 8, "But I will defend my house." The judgment of God is a heavy fact, and the details are scary. "The Lord will take away [Tyre's] possessions and destroy her power . . . , and she will be consumed by fire. . . . Gaza will writhe in agony, and Ekron too. . . . Foreigners will occupy Ashdod . . . " (9:4-6). It is a picture of judgment coming down all around God's people. Yet in the middle of all of it, "I will defend my house against marauding forces. Never again will an oppressor overrun my people, for now I am keeping watch" (9:8). When the action begins, hold on to the promise of protection!

The lands of Hadrach, Damascus and Hamath are what we know today as Syria. "The word of the LORD is against" them (9:1). Tyre and Sidon were the major cities of Lebanon, and they fell under the same judgment. They may have looked blessed because of their wealth but the Lord had lifted His hand against them. Because we have watched that beautiful land self-destruct in recent years, we can sense the force of the prophecy.

In their time, the Phoenicians of Tyre and Sidon were the merchants of the Near East. Their ships went all over the Mediterranean and the Atlantic coast of Europe. Their business was commercial transit between East and West, and they became very wealthy. In the twentieth century, Lebanon has had much the same role. The modern Lebanese have been the commercial people of the Eastern Mediterranean who brought together the buyers and sellers of Europe and the Arab world. They introduced Western progress to their xenophobic neighbors, and they offered the charm of the Middle Eastern cultures to grace European tastes. This blend and their prosperity made Beirut the Jewel of the Levant. It is certainly not much of a jewel now. A long civil war has destroyed this charming city, and the divisions that rend that land have left it impoverished. The prophet said the destruction of the cities of Lebanon is because the word of the Lord is against them. He said that everyone would be on edge watching the region closely, as if with an anxious sense of the ominous, an instinct that perhaps God may be at work in these developments fulfilling this prophecy.

Gaza, Ekron, Ashkelon and Ashdod will be devastated. These cities of the Philistines stood in the area we call the Gaza Strip. The prophetic word was that the hand of the Lord would be against these people, and the description of their fate is harsh. All of this was uncomfortably close to home. If disaster overtakes our near neighbors, are we sure to fall too? But the encouragement follows quickly: "I will defend my house against marauding forces" (9:8).

Everything in the first seven-and-a-half verses of chapter 9 was remarkably fulfilled in the fourth century B.C. One hundred and fifty years after Zechariah recorded this oracle, Alexander the Great suddenly appeared in the region. None but Daniel, it seems, could have imagined the end of the Persian Empire. But when Alexander emerged, the Persian power was destroyed in three years.[2] If we had been there we could have followed the local news in 333 and 332 B.C. by going from one verse to another in Zechariah 9.

In the late fall of 333 B.C., Alexander defeated the Persians at Isis in Asia Minor. He then sent General Parmenio to take Damascus. In ancient warfare, a city was besieged until it was starved into submission, a process that usually took many months and sometimes several years. In this case, within days someone on the inside betrayed the city, opened the gates to the Greek general, and Syria was overrun almost overnight. Alexander had not yet arrived when verse 1 and the first half of verse 2 were already fulfilled.[3]

Alexander turned directly to the city of Tyre, which was the gateway to the south and Egypt. None in the region expected he would get any farther south because Tyre was absolutely formidable and he wouldn't want to go on with this powerful city at his back. Some of the city was strung along the coastline, but the heart of this great capital of commerce was on an island just offshore. The Phoenicians were fortified there so that none could reach them. They built a breakwater around their island that was 2,460 feet long and twenty-seven feet thick, so that hostile ships without knowledge of the approaches could not reach them. Tyre's extensive fleet and worldwide allies could provision them indefinitely. The great Nebuchadnezzar had besieged the city for thirteen years before giving up. "Tyre has built herself a stronghold; she has heaped up silver like dust, and gold like the dirt of the streets," the prophet said (9:3).

When Alexander arrived, he immediately ordered that everything on the mainland be torn down and thrown into the ocean. He turned his soldiers into slaves to build a causeway half a mile long to reach the island city. Within months he had completely destroyed the mighty Tyre.[4] Their history had been written in advance—Damascus first, verses 1 and 2, then Tyre, verses 2-4.

Suddenly, all of the Philistine cities knew they were next. The prophecy says, "Ashkelon will see it and fear" (9:5). When the Greeks came to the Philistine cities, they all simply surrendered to Alexander, except Gaza, which resisted and was stormed in November 332 B.C., after a two-month siege. Some of these cities were depopulated, others were filled with Greek colonists. Quite a number of Philistines ran over into Judah and in fact became Jews to escape this. They were assimilated into the Jewish people just like David assimilated the Jebusites and made their city of Jebus his capital, now renamed Jerusalem.[5] Our story has just walked us through the first seven verses—in one year. Reading the old prophecy, for those folks, was like reading current events.

The key verse of the chapter says, "But I will defend my house against marauding forces" (9:8). The Jewish historian Josephus tells what happened next.[6] After Alexander destroyed Gaza, he wheeled his whole army to the left and marched for Jerusalem. The city could not have been considered a major threat. Nehemiah had rebuilt the wall and cajoled some of the post-exile community to live there (Nehemiah 7:4-5) but it was an off-the-highway provincial shrine. Yet when Alexander was besieging Tyre he had asked the Jews to switch their loyalty to him and to send him provisions, but they had refused. He determined to make an example of them by punishing them severely.

The high priest Jaddua was in great fear as Alexander approached, but the Lord spoke to him in a dream, telling him to go out to meet the great general. He put on his scarlet and purple robe, his bejeweled elegant ephod and the turban with the gold plate on it that said "Holiness to the Lord." All of the other priests wore their linen vestments and the people all wore white when they walked to meet the approaching army. As they came over the crest of a hill, the sunlight illuminated all of those white robes and the entire Greek army stopped in their tracks as if they had seen an apparition. Alexander himself rode on ahead and when he met the high priest he bowed to the ground in front of him. General Parmenio came up to him and protested, "What are you doing? You don't bow to anybody—everybody bows to you!" Alexander replied, "Let me tell you about my dream."

He went on to explain, "When I was still in Macedonia considering how I might conquer Asia, I saw this very man in a vision, dressed in these very robes. He said that he would give me dominion over the Persians, in fact that all of my plans would succeed, but not because of my brilliance and leadership and energy but because of divine favor. This high priest, dressed in these robes, with that ephod on his breast, with that turban on his head and with that gold plate upon it that says, 'Holiness to the Lord'—this man represents the God who gives me success, and I bow to Him."

The army camped there. The high priest and the others took Alexander into the city, where the young conqueror offered a sacrifice to the Lord. He was shown the book of Daniel who had predicted 200 years before that one of the Greeks would destroy the empire of the Persians, and Alexander accepted the responsibility of fulfilling the prophecy.

The next day before leaving, Alexander spoke to the people of Jerusalem saying, "What favor can I show to you?" The high priest took this remarkable opportunity, and asked the conqueror, "Please sir, will you leave us alone to continue under the laws of our forefathers, and would you exempt us from tribute every seventh year?" Alexander agreed. Jaddua next asked that the Jews in Babylon and Media be granted the same privileges. Again the Greek general agreed. He then encouraged some of them to join his army, and promised that those who did would be allowed to observe Jewish scruples.

Josephus reports that after that remarkable day, Alexander found on his travels that people would pretend to be Jews in hopes of receiving the same preferential treatment. Zechariah's oracle had predicted it all: "I will defend my house." This is the promise of protection.

Then we come to the line, "Never again will an oppressor overrun my people" (9:8). This is specific prophetic language that takes us out of Zechariah's world and brings us to end-of-the-age developments that are quickly becoming current for us. The previous fulfillment in Alexander's career of conquest becomes an illustration of another fulfillment yet to come.

There is multiple fulfillment in other prophetic literature. Daniel's description of future events in chapter 11 can be tracked in the third and second centuries B.C., with Antiochus Epiphanes starring as "the king . . . [who] will exalt and magnify himself above every god . . . vent[ing] his fury against the holy covenant" (Daniel 11:36, 30). But before Daniel's prophecy is finished, we find ourselves looking "at the time of the end" (11:40), as if one story had merged into another. It means that the scenario is to be repeated—more completely. Antiochus becomes an illustration of a greater Antichrist yet to appear, and so "those who are wise" (11:33) will be able to warn people about what is really happening, having seen some of the prophecy already fulfilled.

Likewise, Zechariah's prophecy has already been fulfilled, but that was just to give us an illustration of what God will yet do in a greater way. We too will follow current events with a finger on these verses. Expect Syria to be broken. Lebanon will be impoverished or destroyed. The Philistines, perhaps the Palestinians who have taken their name from those previous inhabitants of the Gaza Strip, will writhe in agony, it says, though in the end what is left of them will be assimilated into Israel as followers of the Lord.[7] It isn't much of a stretch to visualize all of this happening in our lifetime, with the Jewish people in the land once again and with the current configuration of hostile neighbors around them.

While it may be tempting to try to identify current developments in the Middle East with specific lines in the prophecy, we should be tentative when we do so. But if the Palestinians are the ones in view here, what is reported in our news needs another perspective. The radical Muslims, members of Hamas and other terrorists, seem to know how to draw the attention of the cameras. But we should also know that a significant minority of Palestinians are members of an ancient Christian community and the faith of some of these is much more than nominal. God is at work among them, though in the pressure of current events, many Christian Palestinians have left the land. It seems from Zechariah 3:7 that God has a special future for the Palestinians. Before the story is finished, the Jewish people will acknowledge the Lord and they will embrace Jesus as their Messiah, "the one they have pierced" (12:10). All believers will be blended together with them as the people of God. "In those days ten men from all languages and nations will take firm hold of one Jew by the hem of his robe and say, 'Let us go with you' " (8:23). In that international congregation, the "Philistines" receive special recognition: "Those who are left will belong to our God and become leaders in Judah" (9:7). The blood of others that had been their food will be removed from between their teeth, and their integration with the Jews will be as thorough as that of the Jebusites whose city became David's capital.

However that may be played out, it should be clear here that the Lord is the One who will bring judgment on these nations, and He is also the One who can effectively insist that His people should not face annihilation in the holocaust of judgment to come. It is His promise of protection for His people, extended here to include those non-Jews who "will belong to our God" (9:7). "Never again will an oppressor overrun my people, for now I am keeping watch" (9:8).

The Promise of Salvation (9:9-10)

The promise of salvation is a twelve-line poem, familiar because it gives us our worship theme every Palm Sunday.

Rejoice greatly, O Daughter of Zion!
   Shout, Daughter of Jerusalem!
See, your king comes to you,
   righteous and having salvation,
   gentle and riding on a donkey,
   on a colt, the foal of a donkey.
I will take away the chariots from Ephraim
   and the war-horses from Jerusalem,
   and the battle bow will be broken.

He will proclaim peace to the nations.
His rule will extend from sea to sea
and from the River to the ends of the earth.
(9:9-10)

If you underline, "See, your king comes to you," "having salvation" and "He will proclaim peace," you have the heart of this sparkling little piece of poetry.

A warrior king would ride on a horse. Alexander the Great came on a horse. Antiochus Epiphanes came on a horse. The great Roman generals, Titus and Vespasian, who tore up the land of Judea in the years after Jesus, came on horses. Robert E. Lee rode the magnificent horse "Traveler." Generals come on impressive horses. Perhaps it was important for the commander to have the horse with the most stamina. More than that, it was important to project the right image. The man on the biggest horse is the biggest man.

But the king in this prophetic picture will ride on a donkey. At first glance this is like the difference between arriving in a cavalcade of limousines or coming on a moped. There seems to be no prestige or even respect in riding a donkey. But Zechariah's congregation would sense something else happening here. In their heritage, judges and prophets rode on donkeys. There is no pretension of personal power here. This will be a man of peace, not a master of political power. His will be a reign of righteousness that will extend over the whole world, and He will not need pomp or military might to establish it. In fact, when He is enthroned, He will abolish all weapons—they simply will not be necessary.

We have tried in recent years to imagine what that

would be like. In 1985, Presidents Gorbachev and Reagan agreed in Geneva that nuclear war should never be unleashed and that there are no victors in such a war.[8] They tried to follow that up in Reykjavik with a decision to do away with nuclear weapons altogether, and for an exhilarating moment we wondered what a world without weapons of mass destruction would be like.[9] When Presidents Bush and Gorbachev signed the START Treaty, agreeing to substantially reduce their nuclear stockpiles, they called it "The Treaty of Hope."[10] But even though the Cold War is over, hope is ephemeral, because we cannot un-invent these weapons. Several volatile nations are apparently seeking to acquire them and they may well be available from North Korea or from the Russian mafia or unemployed nuclear scientists. The arming of the world is a business that sees little real recession. It is not likely that our best leadership and diplomacy will be able any time soon to give us Isaiah's scenario of tanks converted into tractors, and rifles into refrigerators (Isaiah 2:4).

But when Jesus comes He is going to do that. There will be a tremendous disarmament. "He will proclaim peace to the nations" (Zechariah 9:10). His word will be enough to settle disputes that are normally resolved with guns and bombs. Peace will come to the whole world. Isaac Watts took his cue from this verse when he wrote:

> Jesus shall reign where'er the sun
> Doth his successive journeys run;
> His kingdom stretch from shore to shore . . .[11]

That describes a world different from any that has existed since the fall of humanity. But we have an instinct for it. The whole world aches for a just and lasting peace. When Jesus comes, He comes as a man of peace, and so He chose to ride a donkey.

When Jesus was on His way up to Jerusalem, it was His last trip and He knew it. He knew He was going to lose His life when He got there, and He told that to His uncomprehending disciples. But He still wanted to offer Himself publicly to those who would receive Him, so He carefully set up the presentation. At His direction, they got the foal of a donkey for Him to ride. The animal's owner did not understand, but he yielded to the Lord's request. John tells us that the disciples running the errand did not recognize until later how literally they were fulfilling Zechariah's prophecy (John 12:16), but they obeyed His instructions. The people shouted their enthusiasm as this popular prophet rode into the city. But they did not understand either. Jesus must have hoped that this illustrated message about Himself would have been recognized by someone—anyone. Would no one remember one of their favorite verses about the righteous king coming to them riding a young donkey and bearing salvation? But though they shouted their praise, they didn't "get it." Tragically, many people still do not.

The angel's word to Joseph was, "You are to give him the name Jesus [Yahweh saves], because he will save his people from their sins" (Matthew 1:21). "Your king comes to you . . . having salvation" (Zechariah 9:9). The night of His birth, the angels anticipated "on earth peace" (Luke 2:14). "He will proclaim peace to the nations" (Zechariah 9:10). The day after Jesus' triumphal entry into the city, He addressed those who were rejecting Him with this lament:

> O Jerusalem, Jerusalem, you who kill the prophets and stone those sent to you, how often I have longed to gather your children together, as a hen gathers her chicks under her wings, but you were not willing. (Matthew 23:37)

He was overcome with great sorrow because He had come to bring salvation and peace to people who would not accept it.

We live between the ninth and tenth verses of this prophecy in Zechariah 9. Verse 9 has already happened, verse 10 is still in the future. First He came with salvation (9:9). Later He will come to save (9:16). First He came gently (9:9). Someday He will "appear over them; his arrow [flashing] like lightning" (9:14) to impose a peace on the world whether people like it or not. First He came to offer His gift of salvation to those who would receive Him (9:9). When He comes again, He will rescue, He will save from the great battle those who are His (9:16). With the offer of salvation still on the table and the second coming of the King in view, we live in the moment of Joel's urgency:

> Multitudes, multitudes
>   in the valley of decision!
> For the day of the LORD is near
>   in the valley of decision. (Joel 3:14)

The next section describes the stormy conclusion.

As it becomes apparent that "the times of the Gentiles," as Jesus described this period in history (Luke 21:24), are coming to a close, there is more and more urgency about what side of the salvation issue people are on. Isaac Watts took another cue from Zechariah 9 when he urged,

> Joy to the world!
> The Lord is come;
> Let earth *receive* her King. . . .
> (emphasis added)[12]

Here then is the promise of salvation.

I do not miss the long, cold winters of Alberta, Canada. But I must say that some of my happiest memories from growing up there come out of the great blizzards. Once or twice a season, we would be "blown in" for a couple of days—the Lord shredded our "to do" lists and enforced an unscheduled sabbatical break. As a child, I knew that God was bigger than any of us, and that He wanted to remind us of that.

We were well aware, though, that the big storm was very dangerous, and we respected that. The South is home to us now, and when a winter storm came through a few years ago, the number of people who lost their lives was over 240. That never happens in Alberta, though the temperatures are much colder and the north wind much more fierce. The difference is that in Alberta people are ready for it. They understand it. They respect it. They know how to work with it. They are prepared. That is an important lesson in this chapter. It is important to be prepared for the big storm that is about to happen.

The devastation of Hurricane Andrew in August 1992 gave new urgency to Billy Graham's book *Storm Warnings*. With a finger on the book of Revelation and a keen eye on the horizon, Dr. Graham urges careful preparation. This story is a poignant parable of the gravity of the issue:

> Twenty-three years [before Andrew], in Pass Christian, Mississippi, a group of people were preparing to have a "hurricane party" in the face of a storm named Camille. Were they ignorant of the dangers? Could they have been overconfident? Did they let their egos and pride influence their decision? We'll never know.
>
> What we do know is that the wind was howling outside the posh Richelieu Apartments when Police Chief Jerry Peralta pulled up sometime after dark. Facing the beach less than 250 feet from the surf, the apartments were directly in the line of danger. A man with a drink in his hand came out on the second-floor balcony and waved. Peralta yelled up, "You all need to clear out of here as quickly as you can. The storm's getting worse." But as others joined the man on the balcony, they just laughed at Peralta's order to leave. "This is my land," one of them yelled back. "If you want me off, you'll have to arrest me."
>
> Peralta didn't arrest anyone, but he wasn't able to persuade them to leave either. He wrote down the names of the next of kin of the twenty or so people who gathered there to party through the storm. They laughed as he took

> their names. They had been warned, but they had no intention of leaving.
>
> It was 10:15 p.m. when the front wall of the storm came ashore. Scientists clocked Camille's wind speed at more than 205 miles per hour, the strongest on record. Raindrops hit with the force of bullets, and waves off the Gulf Coast crested between twenty-two and twenty-eight feet high.
>
> News reports later showed that the worst damage came at the little settlement of motels, go-go bars, and gambling houses known as Pass Christian, Mississippi, where some twenty people were killed at a hurricane party in the Richelieu Apartments. Nothing was left of that three-story structure but the foundation; the only survivor was a five-year-old boy found clinging to a mattress the following day.[13]

These last chapters in Zechariah are storm warnings. All that some people know to do is to "ride it out" somehow. Others know better and stubbornly refuse to flee to the fortress, as the Lord warns us to do in 9:12. It is time to prepare for the storm. It is urgent that we sound the warning and offer refuge to others too.

Another story from Billy Graham is a joke about a rabbi in Israel who was talking to a group of visiting Christians. In jocular fashion, he said to them, "You know, our two religions are not all that far apart. When the Messiah comes, we'll just ask him, 'Is this your first or second visit?' " Dr. Graham adds, "The humor of that remark cannot disguise the terrible consequences it entails, for when Christ returns, that slight difference will make all the difference in the world for you."[14]

Jesus came with salvation. Peter preached fervently, " 'Repent and be baptized, every one of you, in the name of Jesus Christ for the forgiveness of your sins.' . . . With many other words he warned them; and he pleaded with them, 'Save yourselves from this corrupt generation' " (Acts 2:38, 40).

The Promise of Release (9:11-10:1)

In Zechariah 9:11, God's people are "prisoners." By verse 16 they are "jewels in a crown." In this block of verses is the promise of release. "I will free your prisoners from the waterless pit" (9:11).

Imagine yourself in a waterless pit. We saw an ancient grain storage pit in Israel, perhaps thirty feet deep and eighteen feet wide, circular and lined with stone. When it was not needed for grain, it was the community jail. Remember Joseph held in a pit? (Genesis 37:23-28). He wasn't the only one. Jeremiah was detained in a pit without a solid bottom, and he sank into the muck. He would have died there if not for the special intervention of Ebed-Melech (Jeremiah 38:6-13). Sometimes life is a waterless pit—a prison, a box of unfair circumstances. Like Joseph, we can only do our best to live with it until the Lord intervenes to lift us out and give us a life with royalty. Sometimes life is an orphanage, where the whole world groans waiting for adoption (see Romans 8:22-23).

But a promise is extended here "because of the blood of my covenant with you" (Zechariah 9:11). God promises to free His people from the waterless pit.

There is a sense in which a lot of what God has for us is on hold. We have His Spirit, but that is only a down payment, a pledge of our future inheritance. We are promised that our prayers will be answered and our mountains will be moved. But the most substantial of God's promises will wait for fulfillment until He comes to establish His rule of righteousness and peace. We live in a world where our freedom is constricted, but we have been given a taste of the future and we are optimistic people. We may be prisoners, but we are "prisoners of hope" (9:12). We are careful to live disciplined and godly lives because "we wait for the blessed hope—the glorious appearing of our great God and Savior, Jesus Christ" (Titus 2:13). There will come a time when "the LORD will appear over them" (Zechariah 9:14), and we will all be released. The promise is clear.

Since that is where all of this is going, the description in these verses of "that day" takes on special interest. It is encouraging to know about the rescue plans which come in six promises.

1. The Jewish people will return to the fortress, to the land. The Ephraimites, those who were thought to be so totally lost that God could never find them again, will fill His bow. They will return to the land and, eventually, to the Lord (9:12-13).
2. Their prosperity will be double what it was before. There is a remarkable agrarian revolution in the land of Israel today. They are strikingly more prosperous than all of their neighbors. In light of this prophetic word, it must be recognized as a gift of God (9:12).
3. God's people will stand alone in a desperate confrontation with the entire godless world (9:13).

4. At a critical moment, the Lord will appear over them and He Himself will lead them. The Lord is in the storm! (9:14).
5. Their victory will be smashing, for they will be shielded by the Lord Almighty (9:15).
6. The era of peace that follows will bring wholeness and prosperity to a renewed earth. When the prophet saw it, he erupted into very colorful description (9:16-17).

We have already seen in chapter 8 that the Jews will be joined by people of many nationalities in that great renewal. With this promise of release, we can be prisoners with hope. When it begins to happen, keep your finger on this text. What a radiant conclusion!

We are learning to live with the promises of God. There is encouragement here to know that His intention for us is to make us jewels in His crown. It touches a tender sentiment to think that

> Little children, little children,
>   Who love their Redeemer,
> Are the jewels, precious jewels,
>   His loved and His own.[15]

But here, at the source of that figure, the whole flock—all of God's people—are the jewels who will "sparkle in his land . . . attractive and beautiful" (9:16-17). Some of us may not sparkle much yet, and our beauty is often unrecognized due to our uncut condition and our shabby setting. But someday we will shine. So when life is going nowhere and we are imprisoned in constricting circumstances, or when it seems that life is going somewhere fearful, hold on to this, because you are precious and beautiful to Him. He interrupts our discouraged existence and calls us to a deeper confidence in Him with His promise of protection, His promise of salvation and His promise of release.

Verse 11 says, "Because of the blood of my covenant with you, I will free your prisoners from the waterless pit." Zechariah's audience would recognize this reference to the covenant at Sinai, where it was arranged that their sins were to be covered by the blood of an innocent lamb. Moses took some of the blood from that sacrifice, "sprinkled it on the people and said, 'This is the blood of the covenant that the LORD has made with you' " (Exodus 24:8). The sacrifice was re-enacted every day. There are only two other places in the Bible where that key phrase occurs, so when it does it comes with special force. This oracle is one of them. Those who heard Zechariah use the phrase that day knew that the promise of release was for them because they were covenant people and God's promise was sealed with blood.

Four hundred and fifty years later, Jesus said to His disciples, "This is my blood of the covenant, which is poured out for many for the forgiveness of sins" (Matthew 26:28). He expanded the margins. It is those who have entered into the "new covenant" that will be protected, saved and released. It is because of the blood of His covenant with us that God will release you.

Zechariah 9:13 predicts a great polarization in the world, with God's people on one side and those who are not on the other. Sometimes it seems that the polarization has already begun. When these events begin to happen, many will find themselves on the wrong side of the line, hardened in unbelief and excluded from the protection, salvation, release and peace that Jesus came to give. But the door of the fortress is still open. It is time to prepare for the storm and the great divide, to embrace Christ as Savior and Master, and to enter into the covenant relationship He is extending. "The blood of Jesus, [God's] Son, purifies us from all sin" (1 John 1:7). "See, your king comes to you, righteous and having salvation" (Zechariah 9:9). There is an urgency in this issue because the storm is on the way.

Discussion Questions for Further Study

1. Consider your general view of what is happening in the world. Are you a "life-is-cyclical" person—nothing important ever changes? Are you a detail person—praying for parking spaces? Are you a big picture person—with your eye on the horizon? What general correction in your perspective is being prompted by this reading of Zechariah?
2. The promise of protection in Zechariah is for the Jewish people in the final battle. What other promises of protection has the Lord given us that are equally important to hold onto?
3. When you read about emerging end-time developments, does it give you a nudge to be helping people line up on the right side of the great polarization to come? Who are some of the people you want to see come to the Lord while it is still the Day of Salvation? What can you do about it?
4. Can you identify a time in your life when you felt like you were in a bottomless pit? Or perhaps everything was just on hold? What hope does this

chapter give you, even though you are still limited by your present circumstances?

Endnotes

[1] Walter C. Kaiser, Jr., *Micah-Malachi,* The Communicator's Commentary, vol 21 (Dallas: Word Books, 1992), 286.

[2] F.F. Bruce, *Israel and the Nations* (Grand Rapids, MI: Wm. B. Eerdmans Publishing Company, 1963), 120-121. Alexander was the undisputed master of his father's Macedonian empire by 334 B.C. and in October 331 B.C. his defeat of the Persian army at Gaugamela brought an end to the mighty Persian Empire.

[3] J. Barton Payne, *Encyclopedia of Biblical Prophecy* (New York: Harper & Row, 1973), 457.

[4] Kaiser, *Micah-Malachi,* 367-368; and Kenneth Barker, *Zechariah*, The Expositor's Bible Commentary, vol. 7 (Grand Rapids, MI: Zondervan Publishing House, 1985), 658.

[5] Kaiser, *Micah-Malachi*, 367-368; Barker, *Zechariah*, 658; and Payne, *Encyclopedia of Biblical Prophecy*, 414, 458.

[6] Flavius Josephus, "The Antiquities of the Jews" XI:VIII *The Works of Flavius Josephus*, trans. William Whiston (London: William P. Nimmo, n.d.), 243-245.

[7] Barker, The Expositor's Bible Commentary, 6558-6559.

[8] *Facts on File*, vol. 45, no. 2349 (29 November 1985), 882.

[9] *The 1987 World Book Year Book* (Chicago: World Book, Inc., 1987), 14-15.

[10] "The End of the Arms Race," *Facts on File*, vol. 51, no. 2645 (1 August 1991), 565.

[11] Isaac Watts, "Jesus Shall Reign," *Hymns of the Christian Life* (Camp Hill, PA: Christian Publications, 1978), #439.

[12] Isaac Watts, "Joy to the World," *Hymns of the Christian Life*, #52.

[13] Billy Graham, *Storm Warnings* (Dallas, TX: Word Publishing, 1992), 15-16.

[14] Ibid., 124.

[15] William O. Cushing, "When He Cometh," *Hymns of the Christian Life*, #420.

10

A Future Regathering

Zechariah 10:2-12

The idols speak deceit,
diviners see visions that lie;
they tell dreams that are false,
they give comfort in vain.
Therefore the people wander like sheep
oppressed for lack of a shepherd.

"My anger burns against the shepherds,
and I will punish the leaders;
for the LORD *Almighty will care*
for his flock, the house of Judah,
and make them like a proud horse in battle.
From Judah will come the cornerstone,
from him the tent peg,
from him the battle bow,
from him every ruler.
Together they will be like mighty men
trampling the muddy streets in battle.
Because the LORD *is with them,*
they will fight and overthrow the horsemen.

"I will strengthen the house of Judah
and save the house of Joseph.
I will restore them
because I have compassion on them.
They will be as though
I had not rejected them,
for I am the LORD their God
and I will answer them.
The Ephraimites will become like mighty men,
and their hearts will be glad as with wine.
Their children will see it and be joyful;
their hearts will rejoice in the LORD.
I will signal for them
and gather them in.
Surely I will redeem them;
they will be as numerous as before.
Though I scatter them among the peoples,
yet in distant lands they will remember me.
They and their children will survive,
and they will return.
I will bring them back from Egypt
and gather them from Assyria.
I will bring them to Gilead and Lebanon,
and there will not be room enough for them.
They will pass through the sea of trouble;
the surging sea will be subdued
and all the depths of the Nile will dry up.
Assyria's pride will be brought down
and Egypt's scepter will pass away.
I will strengthen them in the LORD
and in his name they will walk," declares the LORD.

Chapters 9, 10 and 11 of Zechariah are all part of the same oracle. In chapter 9, God's people are "prisoners of hope" (9:12)—prisoners, but not hopeless. Before the end of the chapter we found ourselves in a renewed world, the Lord's beautiful kingdom of righteousness.

Sometimes instead of breeding hope, the promises can create a godly discontent within us. One of God's best gifts is a hunger for what He wants to give. Deep down inside, we have an instinct for our real home, our destiny, our promised inheritance. For the moment, we live in the "not yet" of the story. We are prisoners of circumstances that refuse to change and we will never be perfectly content here. But we have the promise of protection, the promise of salvation and the promise of release.

For some of us, discontentment becomes an unwillingness to wait, a frustration that we have not yet received all the blessings that are to come. When we are told how things will be and, recognizing that our experience is less than that, we become discouraged. We feel justified in nursing an anger barely concealed in sarcasm or cynicism. Seeing imperfections in our spouses, we look for better companions. Disillusioned with faulty political leaders, we feel justified in ripping them with caustic comments. We may even discover that our pastor is not all he could be, so we seek to help him find the exit. Impatience is simple immaturity. It is also a misunderstanding of the promise.

The tension between the promise and current realities is illustrated by the jump between the first two verses of chapter 10. In chapter 9, Zechariah told the people what God wanted to do for them, concluding in 10:1 with a beautiful picture of the Lord's rain in the springtime. Then in the next verse he starts a new theme by reminding them of the failures of their leaders. When Ezra and Nehemiah came to Jerusalem not many years later, they found a community that was spiritually anemic, deeply in need of revival. The oracle shows us how the Lord intends to bridge the gap between the "now" and the "not yet." It ought to encourage our patience since our current disappointments will eventually be left behind.

We Need a Shepherd (10:2)

Leaders *do* make a difference. I share with Toynbee[1] and Churchill[2] the conviction that history pivots around great men and women, people who are not content to be shaped by the events around them but who rise to the challenge of their times and change the world.

The Civil War started in 1861 after the election of Abraham Lincoln. Most Americans would be hard-pressed to name one president between Andrew Jackson and Abraham Lincoln. In those twenty-four years, eight men served in that office: Martin Van Buren, William Henry Harrison, John Tyler, James Polk, Zachary Taylor, Millard Fillmore, Franklin Pierce and James Buchanan. None of them stand out in the American pantheon as "great men," or as candidates for inclusion on Mount Rushmore. Though there was something to respect and appreciate in each of these men, in the years when the country needed a great leader, we did not have one and we blundered into civil war.

It was like that in Israel. In a previous generation, inspired preaching, heroic leadership and the help of God had given them their second temple. Zerubbabel, who led the building project, received a personal message from the Lord: "I have a special place in My heart and My plans for you" (see Haggai 2:23). Joshua, the high priest, was given a place to stand in heaven as the intercessor for his people (Zechariah 3:6-7). Together they were the two olive trees in Zechariah's vision, "These are the two who are anointed to serve the Lord of all the earth" (4:14).

Two generations would pass before Ezra and Nehemiah would appear—outstanding leaders to be sure. But in chapter 10, the nation is in between leaders. The Bible does not give us any record of the leaders during this period—none stood out. Zechariah sought to lift their vision with the promises of God. Then, in response to the disappointment they experienced at not yet enjoying the fruit of the promises, he interrupted the prophetic forecasting to talk about Israel's crooked leaders who could so easily be blamed for the national malaise. It is hard for people to be hopeful when their leaders are spiritually weak, so that is where the Lord begins.

> The idols speak deceit,
>   diviners see visions that lie;
> they tell dreams that are false,
>   they give comfort in vain.
> Therefore the people wander like sheep
>   oppressed for lack of a shepherd. (10:2)

The idols here are *teraphim*. Jacob stole Laban's

family *teraphim*, his private household gods, stirring up a major crisis. "You've deceived me, and you've carried off my daughters like captives in war," he said. "But why did you steal my gods?" (Genesis 31:26, 30). *Teraphim* were thought to connect people with the spirits of their fathers, as if the virtue of their honored ancestors would be bequeathed to them.[3] We see them again in the spiritual wilderness of the Judges (Judges 17:5-6). It seems the Hebrew people held onto these things all those years and when their leadership was weak, there was a strong temptation to reach for a connection with the wise spirits of men of the past. The *teraphim*, they believed, would help them know what greater men would have done in troubled times.

What was the harm? Were these any more than good luck charms? Perhaps they simply helped people to be positive. We smile when we learn that a basketball coach talks to an archbishop, arranging for his favorite priest to accompany the team for a critical NCAA tournament game—for good luck!

We are a little more concerned when we hear that a former president's wife regularly consulted with a favorite astrologer.[4] It makes us wonder if that influenced the president at any time when he faced critical decisions.

In Canada, the land of my birth, the prime minister during the depression and war years was a lifelong bachelor who lived with his mother until her death. With his mother gone, with the Quebecois fiercely resisting participation in the war and countless young men disappearing into the northern forests to avoid conscription, Mackenzie King was in the political fight of his life. When his diaries were released posthumously, we learned about his frequent sessions with a medium who put him in touch with his dead mother so that she could tell him what to do.[5] Now that's spooky! And we shudder.

The leaders of Zechariah's people were like that. The diviners who saw visions and told dreams were using forms left over from Canaanite religion. The Lord did not mince words here. "The *teraphim* speak deceit. The visions are lies. The dreams are false." It was as silly as believing horoscopes and fortune cookies. Their leaders were offering the false hope that spring was just around the corner. In effect, Israel were sheep without a shepherd.

Who your leaders are is very important—nationally and spiritually. In the book of Judges, the spiritual and national fortunes of the people rose and fell with good leadership or with no leadership. The opening line in the song of Deborah sums it up:

> When the princes in Israel take the lead,
> when the people willingly offer themselves—
> praise the LORD! (Judges 5:2)

It is a great thing when you have both leaders that lead and people ready to follow. The point here is that we need a shepherd—and we know it.

The Lord Is My Shepherd (10:3)

While God's words express the concern that Israel's leaders were leading the people astray, His tone expresses hurt, as if He is saying, "Why haven't you come to Me for guidance and leadership? I want to be your Shepherd."

My anger burns against the shepherds,
and I will punish the leaders;
for the LORD Almighty will care
for his flock, the house of Judah,
and make them like a proud horse in battle.
(10:3)

The New Testament writers quoted Zechariah seventy-one times.[6] Though it is one of the most obscure Old Testament books to us, it was one of the most familiar to them. The last line in verse 2 about the lack of a shepherd was in Jesus' mind when He saw the crowds and "had compassion on them, because they were harassed and helpless, like sheep without a shepherd" (Matthew 9:36). Their spiritual leadership was weak, their political leadership was corrupt and He had compassion. In fact, He offered Himself as the Good Shepherd.

John 10 is one of our favorite chapters. It speaks to an inner need and we respond to its warmth: "The sheep listen to his voice. He calls his own sheep by name and leads them out. When he has brought out all his own, he goes on ahead of them, and his sheep follow him because they know his voice" (10:3-4). He says, "I am the good shepherd. The good shepherd lays down his life for the sheep. . . . I am the good shepherd; I know my sheep and my sheep know me. . . . I have other sheep that are not of this sheep pen. I must bring them also. They too will listen to my voice . . ." (10:11, 14, 16).

As much as we love those lines, they were scandalous to the people who first heard them. They knew Psalm 23 as well as we do: "The LORD is my shepherd." So who is this man? They wondered. They knew Ezekiel 34 much better than we do. It looks forward to a time when the Lord will be so fed up with the failure of homemade leadership that has emerged in the nation that He Himself would come back to be their Great Shepherd. Jesus was most provocative when He said, "I am the good shepherd."

The response was mixed. "At these words the Jews were again divided. Many of them said, 'He is demon-possessed and raving mad. Why listen to him?' " (John 10:19-20). When they talked about it again, "the Jews picked up stones to stone him . . . 'for blasphemy, because you, a mere man, claim to be God' " (10:31, 33). It is still true that when Jesus is presented clearly, the crowd will be divided. Either we want Him to be our Shepherd or we don't.

So when the Lord sees His people shepherdless, He feels a deep anger, extends His heart to them in compassion and offers Himself to be their Shepherd. "The LORD Almighty will care for his flock" (Zechariah 10:3). Leaders do matter. But our most important step toward the blessings promised in chapter 9 is making sure that *the Lord* is our Shepherd.

It is a forceful concept in this chapter—more than just a sentimental song about green pastures and quiet waters. There are twenty-seven statements in chapter 10 of what the Lord will do in His capacity as Shepherd. Ken Taylor's paraphrase of Psalm 23 reminds us that, "Because the LORD is my Shepherd, I have everything that I need!" (23:1, TLB). And He will take us to the promised land of chapter 9 blessing. Our current leaders are not going to do that. God wants to take care of us Himself. It is critical that we accept His offer to lead us. (In chapter 11 we will see where the road takes us if we reject Him as Shepherd, and it is sobering.)

Because "the LORD Almighty will care for his flock" (Zechariah 10:3), He will lead us from here to there. Watch this progression:

1. We need a shepherd (10:2).
2. The Lord is our shepherd (10:3).
3. "They will be like mighty men" (10:5).
4. "I will restore them" (10:6).
5. "I will . . . gather them in" (10:8).
6. "They will pass through the sea of trouble" (10:11).

Back to the point at hand, He promised to give them leaders.

"They Will Be Like Mighty Men" (10:4-5)

> From Judah will come the cornerstone,
> from him the tent peg,
> from him the battle bow,
> from him every ruler.
> Together they will be like mighty men
> trampling the muddy streets in battle.
> Because the LORD is with them,
> they will fight and overthrow the horsemen.
> (10:4-5)

The figure here is of the infantry fighting against the cavalry, which in ancient warfare would never work. But God is saying, "I will make these people strong enough to do that." It is like the unforgettable picture on the cover of *TIME* magazine of a single resister standing in front of a column of tanks in Tiananmen Square.[7] That is the kind of leaders that God will give His people. If they allow Him to be their Shepherd, they will be like mighty men.

These leaders will come from Judah. As his father Jacob had predicted, Judah's descendants were the leaders. "Your father's sons will bow down to you. . . . The scepter will not depart from Judah, nor the ruler's staff from between his feet, until he comes to whom it belongs" (Genesis 49:8, 10). So the Messiah was to come from Judah. At that point, the tribe of Judah was more intact than all the others. During the exile, the northern tribes had been scattered and had intermarried—only a few of them even remained in distinct little pockets. But Judah's communities were intact in Egypt and Babylon, and they are the ones who sent some to inhabit the land again. The Hebrew people soon became known as "the Jews." When God says the leaders will come from Judah, He intends them to recognize that it will be from among them that He will provide the cornerstone—a solid leader (the tent peg), a reliable leader (the battle bow)—someone who is ready to lead the charge.

Among the Lord's best gifts to us are leaders. In Romans 12 His gifts are built into our character. In First Corinthians 12 His gifts are given with Spirit filling. In First Peter 4 your gift is simply whatever you have that you can use to serve. But when we come to Ephesians 4 the gifts are people—apostles, prophets, evangelists, pastors and teachers (4:11). He wants to give us good gifts, and they will be "mighty men."[8]

The life of Judas Maccabeus is a remarkable story

of God providing a leader. He stands out in the story of God's people as an illustration of an even greater fulfillment of this prophecy yet to come, just as Antiochus is a precursor of the Antichrist.

In the years after Alexander the Great, his empire broke into four pieces, and the Syrian piece was taken by a dynasty called the Seleucids. They ruled over Palestine and tried to impose their Greek culture on all the people there. Some of the Jews wanted it but most did not. A gymnasium in Jerusalem next to the temple was offensive, but a statue of Zeus in the temple itself was absolutely intolerable. There came to this throne one Antiochus who called himself Epiphanes, "The Enlightened One." Insisting that the stubborn Jews should also be enlightened, he came with his army and with his figure of Apollo to impose modern civilization upon them. He set up the Greek god in the temple and sacrificed swine on the bronze altar to desecrate it. He wanted to destroy their religion while he established his. Then he sent his agents out into every Jewish city or village demanding the sacrifice of a pig on their community altar and forbidding observance of the Sabbath.

When they came to the village of Modine, Matthias, its most prominent resident, refused to comply. They brushed him aside and announced that they would kill everyone there unless someone sacrificed the pig. Some poor peasant, fearful for his life and his wife, stepped forward and performed the revolting ritual. Then out of the crowd came Matthias with a knife in hand, and he killed the man who would so desecrate the altar of God. With that, others lurched forward too and killed the entire party of officials and soldiers that had come from Antiochus. The revolution had begun.

Matthias sent the word out through the whole land, "If anyone be zealous for the laws of his country, and for the worship of God, let him follow me," and they fled to the mountains. Within a few days, they heard of a village where a thousand men, women and children were butchered on the Sabbath day, refusing to comply with the order of Antiochus and refusing to defend themselves in violation of the Sabbath law. The Matthias group decided that God would forgive them if they fought this holy war on the Sabbath.

In the course of time, Matthias died and Judas, his son, took over. Epiphanes was occupied with other pressing business, but he sent General Lysias to wipe out the Jews who would not renounce their religion. He marched into Palestine ready to kill every Jew he found. In the face of that, Judas Maccabeus ("The Hammer") came out of the mountains. Against overwhelming odds, he won every encounter convincingly. He took the city of Jerusalem by storm. He dismembered the image of Apollo, spreading its pieces all over the Kidron Valley. He rededicated the altar that had been desecrated, and that great event is still celebrated annually by the Jewish people as the Feast of Dedication or Hanukkah. The Jews were on the edge of extinction, but God sent them leaders as the oracle promised He would. This is one of his best gifts. And Judea was an independent nation again for 100 years.[9] (Ironically, the second round of Jesus' wrangling with His opponents about His offer to be their Good Shepherd was when He was in Jerusalem to celebrate Hanukkah and their last great leader's triumph.)

If first we must recognize that we need a shepherd, and then we accept the Lord as our Shepherd, we are now encouraged to accept that He will often shepherd us by giving us leaders. That is worth celebrating!

"They will be like mighty men" (Zechariah 10:5). The promise here is for another generation of "mighty men" like David's. When David was a fugitive, many others who were in trouble with Saul joined him. "All those who were in distress or in debt or discontented gathered around him, and he became their leader" (1 Samuel 22:2). They were a rowdy group, but God took those misfits and made them the mighty men of David. They were remarkable. Jashobeam the Hacmonite "raised his spear against three hundred men, whom he killed in one encounter" (1 Chronicles 11:11). And then you have "the Three" who were the most loyal to David and risked their lives breaking through the Philistine lines to draw water from the well in Bethlehem when David was tired and discouraged (11:15-19). Abishai deserves special mention as the commander of the Three, though he was not counted as one of them (11:20-21). Benaiah "was a valiant fighter from Kabzeel, who performed great exploits. He struck down two of Moab's best men. He also went down into a pit on a snowy day and killed a lion" (11:22). In the listing of these champions in the book of First Chronicles, God is saying to His people, "Recognize that one of My best gifts to you is mighty men." Zechariah's oracle promised to give us special people to be our leaders.

What makes some leaders mighty men? The Lord Almighty will "make them like a proud horse in battle. . . . Because the LORD is with them, they will fight and overthrow the horsemen" (Zechariah 10:3, 5). Jabez' remarkable prayer included this important line, "Let your hand be with me" (1 Chronicles 4:10). God will give us leaders who will stand in the street and face the horsemen. How's that for leadership!

"I Will Restore Them" (10:6-7)

> I will strengthen the house of Judah
> and save the house of Joseph.
> I will restore them
> because I have compassion on them.
> They will be as though
> I had not rejected them,
> for I am the LORD their God
> and I will answer them.
> The Ephraimites will become like mighty men,
> and their hearts will be glad as with wine.
> Their children will see it and be joyful;
> their hearts will rejoice in the LORD. (10:6-7)

This is the restoration, the revival, that we seek—the blessings so generously detailed in chapter 9.

The folks who were listening to Zechariah present this word from the Lord would know of the remarkable prosperity in their history. They knew that they were not living with the best blessing God could give them. Abraham and Lot found it necessary to part company because "the land could not support them . . . for their possessions were so great" (Genesis 13:6). There was prosperity in Solomon's time and, "The king made silver as common in Jerusalem as stones, and cedar as plentiful as sycamore-fig trees in the foothills" (1 Kings 10:27).

There are times when the Lord's best blessings for us can only be obtained when we give up pursuing them. Jesus challenged the motive and heart of a rich young man who sought to add eternal life to his collection. When he inquired of Jesus how to do that, Jesus told him to give it all away (Mark 10:21). There is a correlation between our following the Lord and His blessing us along the way. Jehoshaphat was uncommonly blessed, and his biographical entry in Second Chronicles offers this key line: "The LORD was with Jehoshaphat because . . . he walked in the ways his father David had followed" (17:3).

Very often the blessing and the wholeness that God seeks to give is not what we would have planned. His ways are still higher than our ways. With good purpose, He walks us through valleys with shadows, and He feasts with us while we are surrounded by enemies, as much as He leads us in green pastures and by quiet waters. But His ultimate intention is unmistakable: "I will restore them." There had been periods in Israel's history that were rich with blessing. God offered that again to those who would let Him be their Shepherd.

These people had been back in the land for sixty years. They were etching out a poor existence while their cousins in Alexandria and Babylon were becoming wealthy. Where then is the blessing that the Lord has promised? The Jews in Israel today live with the tension of carving out a national existence among hostile neighbors, while their American cousins send them money from the safety of Miami Beach and Skokie. There is an alarming number of Israeli young people seeking to emigrate to the United States these days. The once-compelling vision of building a nation has been lost in the ambiguities of current events. Here then, the word of the prophet is that if they will let the Lord be their Shepherd, He will "strengthen the house of Judah . . . save the house of Joseph . . . restore them . . . have compassion . . . as though [he] had not rejected them . . . answer them . . . [they] will become like mighty men . . . their hearts will be glad . . . their children will see it and be joyful; their hearts will rejoice in the LORD" (Zechariah 10:6-7). They will see it as a work of God. He will do it. Blessing is not a homemade pursuit. It was a standing offer in the fifth century B.C. It is true for the nation of Israel today. It is true for you and me. Let the Lord be your Shepherd if you want to be included in the blessings of chapter 9.

There is a promise here too of the last great restoration or revival. This is specifically for the house of Judah and the house of Joseph. "Their hearts will rejoice in the LORD." That has not happened yet, but that is where all of this is going. The promise to restore them is followed by the promise to gather them in through the sea of trouble.

"I Will Gather Them In" (10:8-12)

"I will signal for them," like a shepherd whistling for his sheep, "and gather them in. Surely I will redeem them." I will buy them back from their bondage. "They will be as numerous as before. Though I scatter them among the peoples, yet in distant lands they will remember me. They and their children will survive, and they will return.

"I will bring them back from Egypt and gather them from Assyria"—literally from those two regions, figuratively from both directions. "I will bring them to Gilead," the Golan Heights, "and Lebanon," because "there will not be room enough for them." I will have to give them some extra room. "They will pass through the sea of trouble; the surging sea will be subdued and all the depths of the Nile will dry up. Assyria's pride will be brought down and Egypt's scepter will pass away. I will strengthen them in the LORD and in his name they will walk" (10:8-12).

Who can deny that we are watching this take shape in this century? There is a sense of God at work in the stories of *Fiddler on the Roof*, *The Exodus* and *Schindler's List*. Boede Thoene's *The Zion Chronicles* and *The Zion Covenant* catch the movement. The ad line reads, "Out of the ashes of the holocaust, a sweeping, historical drama of an infant nation, her brave people, and their struggle for survival against overwhelming odds."[10]

Theodore Hertzl was a Austrian-Jewish reporter at the famous trial of Alfred Dreyfus, a French-Jewish army officer falsely convicted of treason. As Hertzl watched the twisted justice of the whole affair, he developed a settled conviction that if anti-Semitism could be an active force even in an enlightened Western democracy like France, then there was no hope of the Jewish people ever finally assimilating in a non-Jewish society. He organized the First Zionist Congress in 1896, aiming for "a publicly recognized and legally secured Jewish home in Palestine."[11] The movement of Jews back to the land picked up momentum. Among them was a young man from Poland named David Green who arrived in 1906 and immediately dropped his European name to become David ben Gurion.[12]

There have been many confusing setbacks and quite a few great moments since. After the British occupied Jerusalem without opposition during World War I, Lord Balfour formally invited the Jews to the land.[13] The decision of the United Nations in December 1947 to partition the land between Jews and Arabs was startling.[14] I remember very distinctly the first week in June 1967 because I was about to be married. It was the springtime of my life and everything around me was in vivid color. A good friend was helping me fix my old car and we were listening to BBC reports from the Golan. We knew by that night that the Jews had taken Jerusalem, and we knew they would never give it back. I remember thinking, *Lord, it would be great if You came back now, but let me get married first!*

Jesus said, "Jerusalem will be trampled on by the Gentiles until the times of the Gentiles are fulfilled. . . . I tell you the truth, this generation [that sees this] will certainly not pass away until . . . they will see the Son of Man coming in a cloud with power and great glory" (Luke 21:24, 32, 27). The end of the age has begun. It ought to set us on edge. Theodore Hertzl has not done this. David ben Gurion has not done this. It is a movement of God. Of the numerous prophecies in the Old Testament that anticipate the Jewish people restored to their land, this is one of the most direct. "I will . . . gather them in," He said. "They will pass through the sea of trouble." There is a clear allusion here to their passing through the sea once before—the Red Sea, when God parted the waters for them. Perhaps the sea of trouble here is all of the pogroms of the tsars and the genocide of the Nazis, perhaps it is the opposition they have faced in their return to the land or maybe it is the sea of trouble yet to come that Jeremiah called the "time of trouble for Jacob" (Jeremiah 30:7). But before the story is done, "In his name they will walk" (Zechariah 10:12). The Lord is the Shepherd and He will orchestrate the great regathering. We are watching it happen.

The message of chapter 10 is, "The Lord wants to be your Shepherd." The difference between living in the frustration of verse 2 and living in the blessing of verse 6 is whether or not you have received Him as your Shepherd. "I will restore them because I have compassion on them," He says. "Their children will see it and be joyful; their hearts will rejoice in the LORD" (10:6-7).

Discussion Questions for Further Study

1. Do the Bible promises and prophecies make you hopeful or discontented? In what ways can both of these be appropriate responses?
2. On what occasions are you most aware that you need a shepherd?
3. What can the Lord do as your Shepherd that no one else can do?
4. What makes some leaders "mighty men"? What can the Lord do for a leader that would make him or her "mighty"?
5. Consider carefully the connection between following the Lord in obedience and receiving His blessing. Can you think of people who have lost what we would normally call "blessings" because of their lack of faithfulness in following the Lord? Can you think of some whose lives have dramatically taken a turn for the better when they have

turned to Christ? What is at the heart of the promise here that "I will restore them"? What should we expect?

6. The fact that modern Israel exists as a nation is obviously a work of God. How would you support that statement?

Endnotes

1 "Toynbee, Arnold (Joseph)," *Encyclopedia Britannica* (Chicago: 1997), vol. 11, 880. Toynbee examined the rise and fall of 26 civilizations and concluded that they rose by responding creatively to the challenges that faced them under strong leadership. They declined, not when the leadership was no longer strong, but when they were no longer creative.

2 In between his first and second political leadership careers, Winston Churchill wrote articles for various newspapers and magazines that were short sketches of some of the great men of his day—most of whom he had come to know well. In 1932 they were gathered together into a volume entitled *Great Contemporaries* (New York: W.W. Norton & Company, 1932). As always, Churchill had his eye on the key players.

3 J.A. Motyer and M.J. Selman, "Teraphim," *The Illustrated Bible Dictionary* (Downers Grove, IL: InterVarsity Press, 1980), 1535. The connection between divination and ancestor worship is common in animistic societies.

4 Joyce Wadler, "The President's Astrologers," *People Weekly*, May 23, 1988, 107-113.

5 H. Blair Neatby, *William Lyon Mackenzie King: 1924-1932—The Lonely Heights* (Toronto: The University of Toronto Press, 1963), 407; and C.P. Stacey, *A Very Double Life* (Toronto: The Macmillan Company of Canada, 1976), 155.

6 Kurt Aland, et. al., eds. *The Greek New Testament*, 2nd edition (New York: United Bible Societies, 1966), 918.

7 *TIME*, June 19, 1989.

8 David's "mighty men" were celebrated in First Chronicles 11 because, "together with all Israel, [they] gave his kingship strong support to extend it over the whole land" (11:10).

9 The story of the Maccabean revolt is told by Josephus in his *Antiquities of the Jews*, Book XII. A modern retelling of the story is in the first two chapters of D.S. Russell, *Between the Testaments*, 2nd edition (Philadelphia: Fortress Press, 1965).

10 Copy on boxed series of *The Zion Chronicles* by Boede Thoene (Minneapolis, MN: Bethany House).

11 Dan Kurzman, *Ben-Gurion: Prophet of Fire* (New York: Simon and Schuster, 1983), 52.

12 Ibid., 101.

13 Ibid., 121. "His Majesty's Government view with favour the establishment in Palestine of a national home for the Jewish People, and will use their best endeavours to facilitate the achievement of this objective."

14 Abba Eban, *Personal Witness: Israel Through My Eyes* (New York: G.P. Putnam's Sons, 1992), 107-125.

11

A Tale of Two Shepherds

Zechariah 11:1-17

Open your doors, O Lebanon,
so that fire may devour your cedars!
Wail, O pine tree, for the cedar has fallen;
the stately trees are ruined!
Wail, oaks of Bashan;
the dense forest has been cut down!
Listen to the wail of the shepherds;
their rich pastures are destroyed!
Listen to the roar of the lions;
the lush thicket of the Jordan is ruined!

This is what the LORD *my God says: "Pasture the flock marked for slaughter. Their buyers slaughter them and go unpunished. Those who sell them say, 'Praise the* LORD*, I am rich!' Their own shepherds do not spare them. For I will no longer have pity on the people of the land," declares the* LORD*. "I will hand everyone over to his neighbor and his king. They will oppress the land, and I will not rescue them from their hands."*

So I pastured the flock marked for slaughter, particularly the oppressed of the flock. Then I took two staffs and called one Favor and the other Union, and I pastured the flock. In one month I got rid of the three shepherds.

The flock detested me, and I grew weary of them and said, "I will not be your shepherd. Let the dying die, and the perishing perish. Let those who are left eat one another's flesh."

Then I took my staff called Favor and broke it, revoking the covenant I had made with all the nations. It was revoked on that day, and so the afflicted of the flock who were watching me knew it was the word of the LORD.

I told them, "If you think it best, give me my pay; but if not, keep it." So they paid me thirty pieces of silver.

And the LORD said to me, "Throw it to the potter"—the handsome price at which they priced me! So I took the thirty pieces of silver and threw them into the house of the LORD to the potter.

Then I broke my second staff called Union, breaking the brotherhood between Judah and Israel.

Then the LORD said to me, "Take again the equipment of a foolish shepherd. For I am going to raise up a shepherd over the land who will not care for the lost, or seek the young, or heal the injured, or feed the healthy, but will eat the meat of the choice sheep, tearing off their hoofs.

"Woe to the worthless shepherd,
who deserts the flock!
May the sword strike his arm and his right eye!
May his arm be completely withered,
his right eye totally blinded!"

Those who spread their clothes and palm branches on the road to celebrate Jesus' arrival at the Passover feast were the living fulfillment of the prophecies of Zechariah. In chapter 9 we read, "Rejoice greatly, O Daughter of Zion! Shout, Daughter of Jerusalem!" And they did! "See, your king comes to you, righteous and having salvation, gentle and riding on a donkey," in fact, more specifically "on a colt, the foal of a donkey" (9:9). John noted that they had not remembered what Zechariah had said about the Messiah king presenting Himself as a man of peace on a donkey (John 12:16). It is clear that many of those who were part of that drama may have recognized Jesus as a righteous man, but they did not realize that He came "having salvation." They were there for the event, but they did not understand the purpose, and they did not remember or understand what Zechariah had said. They missed a critical fulfillment of prophecy.

Zechariah 11 is beautiful Hebrew literature, rich in figures of speech, but obscure to our modern ears. So we wonder about the thirty pieces of silver in 11:12-13, the familiar ring of these words sounding very much like the story of Judas. We read in 11:8-9: "The flock detested me, and I grew weary of them and said, 'I will [no longer] be your shepherd,' " and we may be tempted to wonder when the Lord may grow weary of us and give up on us too. Or we read in 11:16, "I am going to raise up a shepherd over the land who will not care for the lost, or seek the young, or heal the injured, or feed the healthy, but will eat the meat of the choice sheep, tearing off their hoofs," and we wonder when and how that chilling prophecy will be fulfilled. Sadly this chapter was obscure to Jesus' generation too, and they blundered into the mistake that was predicted here.

As the prophetic pieces have accumulated in the book, the composite picture of God's intention for His people has become increasingly forceful and specific. By chapters 10 and 11, the hints of His plans for blessing in chapter 1 are fully developed. But at the same time another theme emerges. At first the warning was only implicit, then it came in larger bites. It was a pointed sermon in chapter 7, predicting tragic events to come. Are those two themes contradictory—predicting a future that is both prosperous and fearful? Does God love His people or does He not? Are these the alternate futures in Moses' warning in Deuteronomy 30, or will both happen, either simultaneously or in succession?

There are very encouraging and very fearful lines in New Testament prophecies as well. It is important to try to sort them out and to learn from this tragic chapter—especially since we are inclined to prefer reading the promises. We easily join the parade on Sunday; sometimes what happens on Friday finds us choosing something else. The warning chapters bear as much import as the blessing chapters.

The ninth chapter presents the king who comes with salvation. The tenth chapter is about what will happen to those who receive Him. The eleventh chapter is about what will happen to those who do not, and it is to this that we now turn our attention.

First we have a poem, then the script for a drama and finally another poem.

1. A Poem: The Day of Ruin Has Arrived (11:1-3).
2. A Drama: His Own Received Him Not (11:4-16).
   - Act One: God Gives a Good Shepherd (11:4-8a).
   - Act Two: God Grows Weary of Them (11:8b-14).
   - Act Three: God Gives Them a Worthless Shepherd (11:15-16).
3. A Poem: The Curse of the Worthless Shepherd (11:17).

A Poem: The Day of Ruin Has Arrived (11:1-3)

The first poem is a lamentation. When we grieve, we think it is virtuous to be strong and dignified, to avoid breaking down. In the Middle East, both ancient and modern, people are encouraged to express their grief—loudly. So we read, "Wail . . . wail . . . listen to the wail . . . listen to the roar . . . ." It is a picture of disaster in the lands that are peripheral to Israel—Lebanon, Bashan and the Jordan Valley. The cedars of Lebanon, the proudest of trees, will fall. The oaks of Bashan, the strongest of trees, will be cut down. And the rich growth of the Jordan, more lush than any other in the region, will be ruined. This is a prophetic picture of judgment that will destroy the nations around Israel. So the poem announces that the day of ruin has arrived.

Chapter 10 is about the Lord regathering the Jewish people and establishing them in strength. Chapter 11 begins with a prophecy of disaster for some of their enemies. The people in Zechariah's audience, whose nationalism had been crushed and suppressed, were liking this message better all the time! Victory was finally in sight! But what comes next is a surprise. The main theme of the chapter is that disaster is coming to the Jewish nation too.

The prophet Amos preached a powerful sermon in which he relayed the Lord's words: "For three sins of Damascus, even for four, I will not turn back my wrath" (Amos 1:3). Then he ripped Damascus with a strong prophetic word, and everybody in his audience likely cheered, "All right! Give it to those Syrians!" Then Amos shouted: "For three sins of Gaza, even for four, I will not turn back my wrath" (1:6). We can envision enthusiastic Jews cheering their response: "We can count more than three or four sins of the Philistines. Let 'em have it! They really deserve the judgment that they're going to get!" Next Amos thundered: "For three sins of Tyre, even for four, I will not turn back my wrath" (1:9). And his audience heartily agreed and shouted back, "Those Phoenicians are terrible blood-sucking merchants. Get rid of 'em!" Then Amos pounded the Edomites and others. We can imagine the excitement in the crowd: "Yes, the Edomites and the Ammonites and the Moabites—God damn them all!"

They were enthusiastically with him by the time he got to the real point: "For three sins of Judah . . . for three sins of Israel, even for four, I will not turn back my wrath" (2:4, 6). Their mental whiplash must have been almost physically painful! "What are you talking about, Amos?! We are God's people! Don't talk to us about judgment. Talk to those sinners about judgment. We've been saved. We've been baptized. We're good Christians. We believe in the Bible. Hey, we even tithe! God has promised to prosper us. And the Bible says that when things get real hard, He will take us all right out of here. So go preach your word of judgment to secular humanists and feminists and new-agers and homosexuals!"

But if God's judgment is real, it is going to be consistent. If His standards apply to our neighbors, they also apply to us. Under God's judgment, the proudest will not stand (the cedars of Lebanon), the strongest will not survive (the oaks of Bashan) and the richest will be ruined (the thickets of the Jordan).

Today the land of Lebanon is no longer a forest. The cedar that prominently graces the flag may be the only one in the country! The last of the great cedars disappeared in the late nineteenth century when the Ottoman Turks decided to build railroads to hold their fragile empire together and they took what was at hand to make railroad ties.[1] The country is a desert. One wonders why the sectarian militias there fight over it so vigorously. Joan and I have been to Bashan—the Golan Heights and northwestern Jordan. It is very bleak. Forests of oaks? There is hardly a tree up there—it is so different from the biblical picture! I remember when we first saw the Jordan Valley wondering what was so attractive to Lot. Jericho is an oasis at a sweet water spring, and there is some natural green at the upper end of the valley. But most of the Jordan River has been diverted. Most of what grows in the valley is irrigated. The water under the famous Allenby Bridge is just a trickle. "Lush" doesn't describe it in any way.

This prophecy about the pride, strength and lushness of Israel's neighbors has been fulfilled. They have been denuded—stark symbols of the judgment of God. As the chapter continues, they become illustrations of what can happen to anyone who rejects the Shepherd—including God's people.

A Drama: "His Own Received Him Not" (11:4-16)

The prophet Jeremiah wore the yoke of an ox the day he preached, "Bow your neck under the yoke of the king of Babylon; serve him and his people, and you will live" (Jeremiah 27:12). It was not a popular sermon, but the Israelites got the point. One of Ezekiel's dramatic messages had him shaving his head and beard, burning a third of it, chopping up a third of it with a sword and throwing the rest to the wind, except for a few strands that he tucked away in the folds of his garment. He certainly had their attention! Then he explained that his actions were an allegory of the nation's future (Ezekiel 5). Again, it was not a very popular message. Neither is this one in Zechariah 11, which was also given in dramatic form.

The Lord was the Director of this production. He cast Zechariah in two roles, first as a good shepherd for His people. It is clear from the beginning that the play is a tragedy. The first few verses sketch a backdrop scenario that would have been familiar. The people were being abused by leaders who were getting rich at their expense. That much is not hard for us to imagine either. Next the Lord declared that He was about to withdraw His help and protection. Perhaps those words did not reach them very deeply, living as they did with regular memorials to remind them that the glory had long since departed. It is not a warning that strikes us with much fear either, but for the opposite reason. We have lived with multiple layers of the blessing of God for generations and we assume it is our irrevocable birthright.

After introducing the fact that Israel clearly needed a shepherd, the prophet put on the clothing and took up the equipment of a shepherd. He acted out God's tender care, particularly to the oppressed of the flock. His two staffs symbolized God's promises of favor and union. They had felt His disfavor for so many years that a hard life had become the norm, the favor of God a remote memory and a yet more remote hope. Their unity too seemed impossibly distant from what they could ask or think. The united kingdom had split in two 450 years previous to this. Now the people of the northern tribes were scattered beyond hope of tracking or recall. Those from Judah and Benjamin who were not taken all the way to Babylon by Nebuchadnezzar, including Jeremiah, had been dragged down to Egypt, whether they wanted to go or not (Jeremiah 43:4-7). A few thousand had returned to the land, but after sixty years without much news to report, God's favor and the old dream of national reconstitution and union were almost hopelessly beyond reach. Now in the drama, the Lord sends to them a shepherd, with His favor in one hand and His promises in the other. The script says that in one month he "got rid of the three shepherds" (Zechariah 11:8). He threw out those who were giving them such terrible leadership.

Zechariah's enactment communicated that God would one day give Israel a good shepherd. Earlier in this very oracle the Lord had said to them, "My anger burns against the shepherds, and I will punish the leaders; for the Lord Almighty will care for his flock, the house of Judah, and make them like a proud horse in battle" (10:3). "My anger burns . . . I will punish . . . the Lord Almighty will care . . . ." His first direction is, "Pasture the flock marked for slaughter" (11:4).

When Jesus came to them, He often explained Himself in prophetic terms. Most frequently He called himself "The Son of Man," a dominant figure in one of Daniel's visions (Daniel 7:13), a more precise explanation of His identity than the distorted "Messiah" figure of their expectations. Returning to His home town of Nazareth, He read from the Isaiah scroll about the Servant of the Lord, and then told the people gathered in the synagogue that the prophecy was fulfilled in Him. They admired His delivery but refused to accept Him as the One God promised. Jesus pungently observed that historically Gentiles had received the Word of the Lord better than the Hebrew people, and with that they tried to throw Him off a cliff (Luke 4:16-30). Jesus was challenged for healing a blind man on the Sabbath and the Pharisees questioned who He was. His response was, "I am the good shepherd,"—in language drawn directly from a familiar psalm and from Ezekiel and Zechariah's prophecies (John 10:11).

When He rode into the city on the donkey surrounded by the acclaim of so many, He was bringing them God's blessing, God's favor and the fulfillment of God's promises. He rode around the southern shoulder of the Mount of Olives, through the Kidron Valley and up through the Golden Gate right into the temple grounds. He immediately began disrupting the business of the "robbers" He found there—the currency people who were getting very rich by providing the required temple coinage in exchange for their profane Roman money so that the pilgrims' dues could be paid with an acceptable currency. For three years He had scornfully poked at the nation's spiritual leaders, but this time He took them on directly. He tangled with the Sadducees who included the priests—the formal religious leaders of the nation. He affronted the elders—the traditional leaders and keepers of the traditions. And He clashed more sharply than ever with the Pharisees—the leaders of the dominant religious party. Those three groups were always bitterly at odds with each other, and it was a rare event when they agreed on anything. But they came together in a pact to get rid of Jesus (Matthew 27:41). He took them all on. He ridiculed them sarcastically, He confounded and embarrassed them in public, and the people thought it was wonderful.

It all followed the pattern of the prophetic drama. God gave them a Good Shepherd who intervened when He saw them being fleeced. He offered them a renewal of His favor. He demolished the pretensions of their three inept spiritual guides. The moment of truth was at hand. Would they now receive Him?

Act Two begins with harsh lines: "The flock detested me, and I grew weary of them and said, 'I will not be your shepherd. Let the dying die, and the perishing perish. Let those who are left eat one another's flesh' " (Zechariah 11:8-9). Within forty years of the rejection of Jesus, all of that was literally fulfilled.

"Then I took my staff called Favor and broke it, revoking the covenant I had made with all the nations. It was revoked on that day, and so the afflicted of the flock who were watching me knew it was the word of the LORD" (11:10-11). God's covenant with the nations prevented them from hurting His people (see Hosea 2:18; Ezekiel 34:25). In having Zechariah break the staff of Favor, God was removing His special protection for them. In 66 A.D. "the afflicted of the flock who were watching me," the followers of Jesus, recognized that what was happening in Jerusalem was the Word of the Lord, exactly as Zechariah had predicted. They remembered Jesus' specific instructions, and they escaped to live in Pella in the Trans-Jordan.[2]

"I told them, 'If you think it best, give me my pay; but if not, keep it.' So they paid me thirty pieces of silver" (Zechariah 11:12). In other words, "If you don't want Me to be your Shepherd anymore, discharge Me for what you think I'm worth." Under the ancient Levitical law, thirty pieces of silver was the fixed rate of compensation for the accidental death of a slave (Exodus 21:32). In Jesus' time it was pocket change, and so the prophet says with biting sarcasm, "the handsome price at which they priced me!" This is settlement money for a dead slave. It is contemptuously little. What can be done with thirty pieces of silver? "And the LORD said to me, 'Throw it to the potter.'. . . So I took the thirty pieces of silver and threw them into the house of the LORD to the potter" (11:13). The potters were there to sell cheap souvenirs to the pilgrims. "Throw it to the potter" is a colloquial expression that means the amount is so little it is insulting. "And if it is too troublesome for you to pay me what you think I'm worth," the Good Shepherd said, "keep it! Don't bother!"

Matthew's Gospel tells us that Judas was seized

with remorse. Pitifully he came back to the chief priests and the elders and tried to undo what he had done. He threw the thirty pieces of silver back at them which clattered on the temple floor. They did not want to undo their deal, and they did not want to put the silver back in the treasury because they said, "it is blood money" (Matthew 27:6). The rationalization here is amazingly ingenious. They could hand Jesus over, asking for His blood, but they certainly would not defile their collection box with blood money. They would put it into a fund that would buy a field from a potter to be used as a burial place for foreigners, who of course could not be buried in a consecrated graveyard, so it did not matter if the money was tainted. Somehow that took care of all their scruples of conscience, but they completely missed the irony in the details. They were so determined to get rid of Jesus that they did not recognize how tragically they were filling the dramatic role as Zechariah's opposites in a play that had been written for them 400 years before.

Next Zechariah broke the "second staff called Union, breaking the brotherhood between Judah and Israel" (Zechariah 11:14). There was no hope left for them to inherit all of the promises of renewal that God had held before them, eager that they would return to Him.

Jesus acted out a Last Supper drama with the same plot. He broke the bread and said, "This is my body given for you" (Luke 22:19). On the cross the next day, He was physically broken. But His body was not the only thing broken that day. Many witnesses of His crucifixion had not received Him, and for them the staff of the Good Shepherd labeled "Favor" (or blessing) was broken, as well as that labeled "Union" (or promise). Many who waved branches and sang His praise just days before lost the blessing He came to give. Having only a passing interest, they grew tired of Him. The Lord said in the prophet's biting monologue, "I grew weary of them" too (Zechariah 11:8).

Malachi was another man God called to speak for Him at a time when His people lacked heart in acting out their religious traditions. He used very hard language about the priests sniffing contemptuously at their religious duties. The people brought crippled and diseased animals as their offerings, keeping the best for themselves (Malachi 1:6-14). They gave to the church what wouldn't sell at the garage sale. When we fall into that, we may find that a prophet steps forward with this same challenging message for us. "You people love the promise chapters, the blessing sermons. You say all the right words about the Lord as your Shepherd, when in fact you are a miserable people to try to shepherd. You are here for the green pastures and quiet waters, but your protests about the rod and staff, about the valley with the shadows and about your table set among enemies reveal your real heart. You are a people marked for judgment. You are so careless spiritually that even when the Good Shepherd that Ezekiel promised arrives in person, you will not receive Him." That is the message here.

In fact, Zechariah kept preaching like that until one day as he stood before them between the bronze altar and the door of the temple, the site of their busy religious duty, someone stepped up and murdered him in the full view of them all. Jesus' words for the teachers of the law were equally assaulting:

> You snakes! You brood of vipers! How will you escape being condemned to hell? Therefore I am sending you prophets and wise men and teachers. Some of them you will kill and crucify; others you will flog in your synagogues and pursue from town to town. And so upon you will come all the righteous blood that has been shed on earth, from the blood of righteous Abel to the blood of Zechariah son of Berekiah, whom you murdered between the temple and the altar. I tell you the truth, all this will come upon this generation. (Matthew 23:33-36)

Jesus was saying that the judgment of God was going to come down on them, that the prophecy of Zechariah 11 would be fulfilled in their lifetime.

> O Jerusalem, Jerusalem, you who kill the prophets and stone those sent to you, how often I have longed to gather your children together, as a hen gathers her chicks under her wings, but you were not willing. Look, your house is left to you desolate. For I tell you, you will not see me again until you say, "Blessed is he who comes in the name of the Lord." (23:37-39)

The crowd that had ushered Him into the city just the day before had used those very words to acclaim Him. Now He is telling their leaders, "I will not come to you again until you too are willing to receive Me."

The alternative is not, as we vainly wish to think, that we do not need a shepherd, that we can do what we want. The alternative is that God will give us a foolish shepherd who will tear off our hoofs.

In the third act of the play, Zechariah changes roles.

> Then the LORD said to me, "Take again the equipment of a foolish shepherd. For I am going to raise up a shepherd over the land who will not care for the lost, or seek the young [wandering], or heal the injured, or feed the healthy, but will eat the meat of the choice sheep, tearing off their hoofs." (Zechariah 11:15-16)

God wants to be the Shepherd of His people. But when they turn away from Him, another shepherd will lead them into a dreadful ruin.

It was the first century A.D. and the Roman General Titus was on the march. He brought major legions from Alexandria up into Judea, encamping at Caesarea to finish his preparations. The Jewish war was in its third year. Vespasian, his father, replaced Nero as emperor and gave Titus the task he himself had begun. Because of their inveterate insolence, the Jews were to be destroyed.[3]

Jerusalem was controlled by the Zealots. Two rival Zealot leaders, John of Gischala and Eleazar son of Simon, drew around them private militias—armed groups who terrorized the city. There were stacks of dead bodies in the streets. No one was safe.[4]

Then the Romans arrived and the siege began. Jesus had predicted the destruction of the city and told His disciples:

> When you see Jerusalem being surrounded by armies, you will know that its desolation is near. Then let those who are in Judea flee to the mountains, let those in the city get out, and let those in the country not enter the city. For this is the time of punishment in fulfillment of all that has been written. How dreadful it will be. . . . (Luke 21:20-23)

His instructions had been clear, the circumstances were unambiguous and His followers were dispersed.

The results of the siege were dreadful. Josephus very graphically described the horror. The brutes who controlled the city killed the wealthy citizens and confiscated their money. Others were tortured until they revealed the location of their food reserves. Those who were caught foraging for food outside the city walls, sometimes more than 500 a day, were tortured and crucified. Some decided to escape certain death in the city and, though sentries were posted with orders to cut the throats of any who tried to escape, there were those who desperately made the attempt anyway. If they made it, their distended bellies and emaciated limbs bore testimony to their utter distress. The Romans cynically encouraged them to eat, giving them as much as they wanted. Most unwisely gorged themselves and died an agonizing death within hours. Then someone discovered a few gold coins in the excrement of a Jewish refugee. Word quickly passed among the soldiers and Arabs in the camps and in one horrible night, 200 Jews were ripped open in a mad gold rush. In the city the people were so weak with starvation that many died digging graves for others.[5] The destruction was complete and merciless.

Zechariah's prophecy is as dreadful as Josephus' description:

> They will oppress the land, and I will not rescue them from their hands. . . .
>
> Let the dying die, and the perishing perish. Let those who are left eat one another's flesh. . . .
>
> I am going to raise up a shepherd over the land who will . . . eat the meat of the choice sheep, tearing off their hoofs. (11:6, 9, 16)

Jesus wept over the city that would not receive Him as their Good Shepherd because He knew what would happen to people who insisted on going on their own, forfeiting the blessing and favor of God.

A Poem: The Curse of the Worthless Shepherd (11:17)

> Woe to the worthless shepherd,
> who deserts the flock!
> May the sword strike his arm and his right eye!
> May his arm be completely withered,
> his right eye totally blinded! (11:17)

There is only judgment at the end of the road for the leaders who led God's people astray and for those who followed them. The judgment the Jewish people have borne all these years is a deep spiritual blindness introduced by centuries of legalism and reinforced by rigid teachers who are largely ignored by most Jews today. The Jewish population is bound together not by their spirituality, but by a strong sense of kinship and tradition forged through centuries of grief and an instinct for survival. Most are secular people having lost a once profound relationship with God. It is a sad story and this is a sad chapter. But it is not the last chapter! The second oracle, chapters 12-14, outlines a dramatic intervention of God yet to come.

* * *

The city was crowded with Jews from the Diaspora, and they were amazed that these men and women could speak their languages. Many others who were there that day had been in the crowd seven weeks earlier calling for Jesus' crucifixion, though they may not have been quite sure why. As if they were participating in the enthusiasm of a great sporting event, they had shouted to Pilate, "Let his blood be on us and on our children!" (Matthew 27:25). Now they were witnessing another preacher with a Galilean accent, remarkably convincing, quoting Scripture, boldly arguing that Jesus of Nazareth was "accredited by God." He thundered, "You, with the help of wicked men, put him to death by nailing him to the cross" (Acts 2:22-23). They had made a terrible mistake. Panic spread among them. They had crossed the pivot point in Zechariah 11. They had rejected the Shepherd and surely God had withdrawn His favor!

Peter went on. "God has raised this Jesus to life,

and we are all witnesses of the fact. Exalted to the right hand of God, he has received from the Father the promised Holy Spirit and has poured out what you now see and hear" (2:32-33). They could see the tongues of fire. They could hear the remarkable translation into so many languages. "God has made this Jesus, whom you crucified, both Lord and Christ" (2:36). And they were cut to the heart. His blood really was on their heads.

Alarm was replaced by dreadful fear, for they knew there was no escape. "Brothers, what shall we do?" (2:37). The answer sounded too good to be true: "Repent and be baptized, every one of you, in the name of Jesus Christ for the forgiveness of your sins. And you will receive the gift of the Holy Spirit" (2:38). Zechariah 10 and 11 will both be completely fulfilled, but they are still alternate futures. The promise was open for Peter's audience and their descendants. Though they had made a disastrous choice, they were invited to move over from the inevitable conclusion of the rejection chapter to the full promise of the blessing chapter. "Save yourselves from this corrupt generation," Peter urged (Acts 2:40). And 3,000 of them did. They stepped over from the way that leads to death into the way that leads to life.

Ironically, the profound discomfort that comes with the provoking presentation of Zechariah, the demanding disputations of Jesus or the damning proclamation of Peter is because of God's calling—calling us to repentance and forgiveness, to baptism and Spirit filling. Here Jesus again urges people to come in out of the cold and gather under the wing that He offered them the day He rode into town on a donkey.

Just over a century ago, two famous strident atheists sat on a train together discussing, of all things, the life of Christ. One of them said, "I think an interesting romance could be written about that." The other replied, "And you are just the man to do it. Tear down the prevailing sentiment about his divinity and paint him as a man—a man among men." The one who made the suggestion was the pugnacious Englishman Charles Ingersoll. The man who took up the project was an American whose name was Lew Wallace, a gentleman who had been a general in the Civil War and then a diplomat in Europe, most notably at the Ottoman Court in Istanbul.

Wallace found himself drawn into the story as he tried to write it. Then he stumbled on two lines. The first one that he could not get away from was Pilate's question, "What shall I do, then, with Jesus who is called Christ?" (Matthew 27:22). The second that he could not avoid was the confession of the man who had nailed Him to the cross: "Surely he was the Son of God!" (27:54). Lew Wallace found that his life was changed. So was his book. He called it *Ben Hur*. It is the story of the centurion and it portrays the tremendous change in a person's life when he or she surrenders to Jesus Christ.[6]

He wants to be your Shepherd. He comes to you with gifts of blessing in His hands. He grieves because He knows what your rejecting Him will lead to. In the end, it will be the difference between Zechariah 11 and Zechariah 10. The choice is yours. What will your future hold? What will you do with Jesus who is called Christ?

Discussion Questions for Further Study

1. What actions and attitudes in our culture deserve the judgment of God? What about in your unbelieving neighbors? And in your life?
2. Imagine life without any of God's blessings. What would be different?
3. What parallels can you draw between the story of Jesus' rejection as the Good Shepherd followed by the account of the worthless shepherds that led the Jewish people into such a horrible tragedy and the world in which we live (and the church in which we worship)? Are similar decisions being made? Where may these decisions lead us?
4. Zechariah 10 and 11 are offered as alternate futures. There is a clear choice each of us must make. What can you learn from the drama of Zechariah and the story of Jesus? Will you decide to allow Jesus to be your Shepherd?

Endnotes

[1] From a tape recording of a tour guide from the author's visit to the railway tunnels in Rosh Hanikra in northern Israel.

[2] Eusebius Pamphilus, *The Ecclesiastical History* III:V (Grand Rapids, MI: Guardian Press, 1955), 86.

[3] Flavius Josephus, "The Wars of the Jews" IV:IV:5; V:I:1, in *The Works of Flavius Josephus*, William Whiston, trans. (London: William P. Nimmo, n.d.), 546-547.

[4] Ibid., 547-548.

[5] Ibid., 564-569.

[6] Paul Lee Tan, "Origin of 'Ben Hur,' " *Encyclopedia of 7,700 Illustrations: Signs of the Times* (Rockville, MD: Assurance Publishers, 1979), 276.

12

The Lord Will Intervene

Zechariah 12:1-13:6

An Oracle

This is the word of the Lord *concerning Israel. The* Lord, *who stretches out the heavens, who lays the foundation of the earth, and who forms the spirit of man within him, declares: "I am going to make Jerusalem a cup that sends all the surrounding peoples reeling. Judah will be besieged as well as Jerusalem. On that day, when all the nations of the earth are gathered against her, I will make Jerusalem an immovable rock for all the nations. All who try to move it will injure themselves. On that day I will strike every horse with panic and its rider with madness," declares the* Lord. *"I will keep a watchful eye over the house of Judah, but I will blind all the horses of the nations. Then the leaders of Judah will say in their hearts, 'The people of Jerusalem are strong, because the* Lord *Almighty is their God.'*

"On that day I will make the leaders of Judah like a firepot in a woodpile, like a flaming torch among sheaves. They will consume right and left all the sur-

rounding peoples, but Jerusalem will remain intact in her place.

"The LORD will save the dwellings of Judah first, so that the honor of the house of David and of Jerusalem's inhabitants may not be greater than that of Judah. On that day the LORD will shield those who live in Jerusalem, so that the feeblest among them will be like David, and the house of David will be like God, like the Angel of the LORD going before them. On that day I will set out to destroy all the nations that attack Jerusalem.

"And I will pour out on the house of David and the inhabitants of Jerusalem a spirit of grace and supplication. They will look on me, the one they have pierced, and they will mourn for him as one mourns for an only child, and grieve bitterly for him as one grieves for a firstborn son. On that day the weeping in Jerusalem will be great, like the weeping of Hadad Rimmon in the plain of Megiddo. The land will mourn, each clan by itself, with their wives by themselves: the clan of the house of David and their wives, the clan of the house of Nathan and their wives, the clan of the house of Levi and their wives, the clan of Shimei and their wives, and all the rest of the clans and their wives.

"On that day a fountain will be opened to the house of David and the inhabitants of Jerusalem, to cleanse them from sin and impurity.

"On that day, I will banish the names of the idols from the land, and they will be remembered no more," declares the LORD Almighty. "I will remove both the prophets and the spirit of impurity from the land. And if anyone still prophesies, his father and mother, to whom he was born, will say to him, 'You must die, be-

cause you have told lies in the LORD*'s name.' When he prophesies, his own parents will stab him.*

"On that day every prophet will be ashamed of his prophetic vision. He will not put on a prophet's garment of hair in order to deceive. He will say, 'I am not a prophet. I am a farmer; the land has been my livelihood since my youth.' If someone asks him, 'What are these wounds on your body?' he will answer, 'The wounds I was given at the house of my friends.' "

It should be clear that the last three chapters of Zechariah describe end-of-the-age developments. It is my conviction that the end of the age and the return of the Lord is near. I believe that it is likely to occur in my lifetime, and I want to explain why I believe that to be so as an introduction to these last two chapters of the book. The fulfillment of this prophecy is sure to be soon.

A few years ago, many people seemed to overdose on prophecy hype. Books on the subject sold millions of copies and sensational preachers assiduously scrutinized current events to discover ever more specific identification of the details of prophecy being literally fulfilled. People acted as if the Lord had given us a cosmic game, the challenge of which was to break the codes in Scripture and in international developments which led to the inside knowledge needed to be well prepared. There were even major movies produced portraying scary scenarios frightening people into making sure they are ready. I agree that we need to know what to expect and that we need to be prepared for it. But it is sad to see that many have reacted to this prophecy frenzy with an agnosticism about future things altogether. "The experts disagree, so nothing is for sure." "I'm not going to worry about it." "It will all pan out in the end." "Don't borrow future trouble." "What's important is what's happening now."

Perhaps that is changing now. There is a general concern about the future. The end of the millennium seems to generate sober reflection. Christians are anxious.

With all of that, we need a source of help and hope. The Lord gave this oracle to Zechariah to give His disheartened people a perspective on life. The apostle Paul wrote to the new and harassed Christians in Thessalonica about the return of the Lord, intending that they should "encourage [or comfort] each other with these words" (1 Thessalonians 4:18).

Paul was concerned that they get it right because distortions of what he had taught them were the source of serious stresses. "Now, brothers, about times and dates we do not need to write to you, for you know very well that the day of the Lord will come like a thief in the night" (5:1-2). That is, you can't predict exactly when, so don't press me for a date. "While people are saying, 'Peace and safety,' destruction will come on them suddenly, as labor pains on a pregnant woman, and they will not escape" (5:3). It is as if the world is pregnant and does not know it. Everyone is preoccupied with his or her own peace and safety, refusing to think of the future. Yet the coming of the Lord is as certain as the birth of a baby, whether you are counting the weeks or not.

"But you, brothers, are not in darkness so that this day should surprise you like a thief" (5:4). The thief-in-the-night surprise will be the experience of those not paying attention. "You are all sons of the light and sons of the day. We do not belong to the night or to the darkness. So then, let us not be like others, who are asleep, but let us be alert and self-controlled" (5:5-6). We have been given light, revelation, knowledge, insight, teaching. It ought to help us keep our balance. We need not be among the surprised because we have been given enough light.

By Dwight Pentecost's count, "one fourth of the books of Scripture are prophetic, and one verse in five deals with something that was prophetic at the time it was written. Since prophecy occupies such a large portion of Scripture, it is crucial that we know how to interpret it."[1] I would add that with the dramatic developments in our world today, it is important for us to pay attention to the news as well.

John Walvoord has written about the detail of prophecy more than anyone in our generation. According to him,

> The significance of the present world crisis is that it contains practically all the elements which are a natural preparation for the end of the age. . . . The present generation may witness the dramatic close of the time of the Gentiles and the establishment of the kingdom of heaven upon earth, thus bringing to fulfillment one of the great themes of prophecy—the divine program for the nations of the world.[2]

With appropriate modesty about what we do not know, let us be sure of what we do know. Five major indicators suggest that the stage is being set for the return of the Lord—prominent developments that fulfill prophetic prediction as never before.

Gospel Witness

The first is gospel witness. Matthew 24:14 says: "This gospel of the kingdom will be preached in the whole world as a testimony to all nations, and *then* the end will come" (emphasis added). That certainly is an answer to the "when?" question. The pace of world witness seems to be accelerating. We have watched the opening of the former Soviet Union with a previously unthinkable suddenness, and the rush of mission activity to reach the people there who have been spiritually deprived for so long. In 1993, Billy Graham's Crusade in Germany was linked by satellite to every country in Europe and several in Africa so that hundreds of millions could hear the gospel at the same time. In January 1994, a similar gospel mission in Japan was heard throughout East Asia. His crusade in Puerto Rico in 1995 used thirty satellites to transmit to 3,000 downlink sites in 185 countries, translating his message into 116 languages. China was the only major area of the world that wasn't connected.[3]

Furthermore, internationalization of the missions movement has given it a tremendous new impetus. Almost 4,000 delegates from 186 countries gathered in Seoul, South Korea in May 1995 for a Global Consultation of World Evangelization, "the largest and most widely representative international gathering in history. And it focused on establishing a church-planting movement within the unreached peoples of the world by the year 2000."[4] According to prominent missiologist, Dr. Ralph Winter, "at no time in history have we been so close to completing the preliminary penetration task of mission effort into all the peoples of the world."[5] A large Presbyterian church in Seoul, South Korea committed to sending one-quarter of its 8,000 members to the mission field. On top of that, the pastor and 800 members have made a lifetime commitment to pray two hours a day for their missionaries and world evangelization.[6]

Missions Frontiers magazine from the U.S. Center for World Mission in Pasadena continues to update our progress. It proclaims in bold print in every issue:

> "The Growth of the Gospel! God Is Building His Church—Rapidly. Across the centuries, Bible-believing Christians have become an ever-larger portion of world population. In A.D. 1430 only one in one hundred was a Bible-believing Christian. Today, one in nine is. This huge body of real believers is growing at the rate of more than three times that of the world population! Christianity is by far the fastest growing global religion. . . ."[7]

And if you are counting people groups that have been penetrated by gospel witness, of the 10,504 that they identify, only 1,873 have no indigenous evangelical Christians among them, and most of those are related to other people groups where there is a Christian presence.[8]

The last major area of resistance is the Muslim world. Communism's collapse makes it possible to believe that Islam's apparent impenetrability is not too hard for God either. In fact, cracks in that great wall are reported with increasing frequency. Millions of Christians are "praying through the window," and there is a distinct rise in initiatives to reach Muslim people. As never before, we can imagine that within our lifetime the gospel will have been effectively presented as a witness to all nations, that the Lord will have gathered from out of every tribe and nation a new people for Himself, and then, as Jesus said, "the end will come" (Matthew 24:14).

Jerusalem Belongs to the Jews

The second major end-of-the-age development is that Jerusalem is in the hands of the Jews again. Jesus plainly said,

> Jerusalem will be trampled on by the Gentiles until the times of the Gentiles are fulfilled. . . .
>
> When you see these things happening [that is, among other things, the end of Gentile rule in Jerusalem], you know that the kingdom of God is near.
>
> I tell you the truth, this generation [i.e., the generation that sees these things begin to happen] will certainly not pass away until . . . they . . . see the Son of Man coming in a cloud with power and great glory. (Luke 21:24, 31-32, 27)

Perhaps, with recent confusing developments, we have forgotten the spine-tingling drama of watching the Jewish Defense Forces reclaim Jerusalem during the Six Day War. They had not owned their capital city for 1,900 years. Israeli national euphoria overflowed the chasm of their centuries-old national grief.

Those of us expecting Christ's return knew that we were watching a pivotal moment in history that signaled the end of the times of the Gentiles. The hand of God was very definitely directing events.[9] We stood in wonder remembering that Jesus had said, "When these things begin to take place, stand up and lift up your heads, because your redemption is drawing near" (Luke 21:28). In other words, expect to see His coming in your lifetime.

The Threat of Nuclear War

Third, unique to this generation is the threat of nuclear war. Second Peter 3:10 reads: "The day of the Lord will come like a thief." There is that line again—it will be a surprise to those who scoff about these things. Then, "the heavens will disappear with a roar; the elements will be destroyed by fire [in fervent heat], and the earth and everything in it will be laid bare." That seemed unlikely and hyperbolic a generation or two ago, but it is not hard to imagine now. Students of prophecy differ trying to place this one in the overall scenario, but with modern developments, the prophetic literature seems less fantastic, more plausible, than ever. If we no longer fear a communist superpower with thousands of nuclear weapons, we twitch a little to think of Iran or North Korea or the Russian mafia collecting a few. The proliferation of possibilities in the new world disorder serve to remind us that the pieces are assembling for end-of-the-age developments.

An Interconnected World

The fourth major indicator is an increasingly interconnected world. A revived United Nations and a new GATT treaty to reduce trade barriers are the orders of the day. Renegade regimes are opposed by countries large and small moving in concert to make the world safe. Robert Reich, the Harvard professor and former Secretary of Labor, is an apostle of the economics of the twenty-first century, envisioning money, technology and jobs flowing freely across borders with corporations losing their national identity.[10]

Zechariah 12:3 has "all the nations of the earth . . . gathered against [Jerusalem]" and the details in chapter 14 are grimly graphic. It should cause us to shudder when we recognize that if a coalition of world forces can come together so convincingly and so quickly against Iraq in 1991, the Bible's prediction that all the nations will come together against Israel is no longer unfeasible.

The European Union

A fifth indicator worth watching is the European Union. Daniel's vision of the large statue seems to indicate that the strong-as-iron Roman Empire will be divided into two legs, and then further into toes. In the end it will be "a divided kingdom; yet it will have some of the strength of iron in it. . . . Just as you saw the iron mixed with baked clay, so the people will be a mixture and will not remain united" (Daniel 2:41, 43). His vision of the beast with ten horns in chapter 7 adds detail to the scenario. The Roman Empire formally split into Western and Eastern or Byzantine halves in 395 A.D., forming the "legs" of the statue.

In Daniel's prophecy, it is apparent that this "kingdom" will be a dominant political factor when "the

God of heaven" smashes the nations and sets up "a kingdom that will never be destroyed" (2:44). Eduard Shevardnadze, as Foreign Minister of the U.S.S.R., engineered some of the major developments that brought East and West Germany and all of Europe together again. One chapter in his book *The Future Belongs to Freedom* celebrates "The New Europe." The "idea of Europe," envisioned two centuries ago by Jean-Jacques Rousseau, was "ripened too early. . . . Now this time has arrived, and for the first time since antiquity the European idea has a chance to be put into practice."[11] Suddenly this is much more than a "Common Market" or a Western alliance against the East. With the iron curtain removed, European unity is potentially much more extensive than those old concepts envisioned, and with 1999 as the target date for a joint currency and unified foreign policy,[12] there is a startling new momentum in the process. While the details in Daniel are not perfectly congruent with the nightly news, we can observe the eagerness of previously skeptical nations to be included, and we wonder where this phenomenon will lead.

Other Pieces of the Puzzle

Besides those five developments which are unique to our times, there are many secondary pieces that are part of the prophetic puzzle. Jesus said that wars and rumors of wars should not be alarming. He was telling His disciples to expect to live in difficult times. Famines and earthquakes in various places, persecution and betrayal, the increase of wickedness and the love of most growing cold are not so much signs of the end as they are characteristics of the sad world to be endured while the gospel is preached to all nations. These calamities are called "the beginning of birth pains," and with that He gave a sense of increasing intensity before an inevitable end (Matthew 24:6-14).

Second Timothy 3:1-5 insists on a similar realism:

> But mark this: There will be terrible times in the last days. People will be lovers of themselves, lovers of money, boastful, proud, abusive, disobedient to their parents, ungrateful, unholy, without love, unforgiving, slanderous, without self-control, brutal, not lovers of the good, treacherous, rash, conceited, lovers of pleasure rather than lovers of God—having a form of godliness but denying its power.

Peter announced that "the last days" had begun with Pentecost (Acts 2:14-17)—it was their language for the age of the Spirit. Perhaps this period of history would be described better as the "latter" days, in contrast to the former days, to avoid our mistaking this as a description particular to end times. Here again Christians are counseled to expect they will be surrounded by people given over to evil, and it has certainly been true all these years. But this chilling note in Revelation suggests an increasing intensity of this evil in the last days of "the last days":

> But woe to the earth and the sea,
> because the devil has gone down to you!
> He is filled with fury,
> because he knows that his time is short.
> (12:12)

In this decade, freedom is breaking out all over the world. While we celebrate this unprecedented advance for one of our most cherished values, a more sober reflection will ask, "Free to do what?" The Timothy verses indicate the natural inclinations many are now free to pursue. These developments are not unique to our generation but they are increasing in intensity.

It seems there are trip wires all over the world, any one of which could launch the events of the end times. National governments continue to borrow massive amounts of money as if government is somehow immune from the crash that results when anybody else does it. Third world countries teeter on bankruptcy. Dictators seek to acquire weapons of mass destruction. Ancient ethnic hatreds erupt caustically and threaten to draw us all in again. Middle Eastern developments are watched by an inordinately large press corps because of our visceral fear that what happens there may lead to Armageddon.

So we watch the news. We must also do our best to understand what we are reading here in Zechariah. Paul wrote that we need not be surprised by any of this when it happens. Zechariah chapters 12 and 13 are the word of the Lord concerning Israel.

* * *

"This is the word of the LORD concerning Israel" (Zechariah 12:1). In the events of the final chapters of history, Israel will again be at the center of the action.

A member of our congregation told me recently of a Palestinian friend who will not consider Christianity because Christians seem to be so pro-Israeli. That can be a pressure point for missionaries to the Arab world too. Even when we shared the euphoria of the Six Day War, Elisabeth Elliot wondered out loud how we could construe what we were seeing in Israel as a work of God when the Jewish people themselves hardly recognize Him, and when their capture of their ancient homelands is such a blatant injustice to the Palestinians.[13]

A preliminary answer to that concern has already emerged in Zechariah 8:20-23, where people from all languages and nations are portrayed as seeking the Lord together. In 9:7 we may be reading about Palestinians merging with the Jews as the people of God, just as the Jebusites did in David's time. God has not forgotten the other nations in His special concern for the children of Abraham.

The longer answer to the concern fills chapters 12-14. There will come a day when the Jews will emerge as the people of God like they have not been since the Lord broke His shepherd's staff called Favor (Zechariah 11:10) because they had rejected the shepherd He sent them. But He will make them strong again; He will come to them once again and this time they will receive Him; He will cleanse them of their sins; He Himself will fight for them. Before the end of the story, we will see the survivors from *all* the nations worshiping Him. If some of what we see in current events strikes us as unfair, consider that the Lord has not yet come to make things right. Read what He plans to do next. It is His intention to finish what He set out to do with the Hebrew people when He promised Abraham that they would be His channel of blessing to all the peoples of the earth (Genesis 12:3).

"This [oracle] is the word of the LORD concerning Israel. The LORD, who stretches out the heavens, who lays the foundation of the earth, and who forms the spirit of man within him . . ." (Zechariah 12:1). First we are challenged to visualize Him creating the world out of nothing with a commanding word. Picture Him throwing the stars into the immensity of space and creating the wonder of life in the infinitely small and wonderfully balanced details of human physiology. Then we will be ready to consider what He says He is about to do next. It will be as miraculous as the first creation!

After chapter 11, where the covenant with Israel was broken off, the God who created us comes to Israel again with a dramatic intervention (12:2-9), a spirit of grace and supplication (12:10-14) and a cleansing fountain (13:1-6).

A Dramatic Intervention (12:1-9)

"Judah will be besieged as well as Jerusalem . . . when all the nations of the earth are gathered against her" (12:2-3). That is the opening scenario. And then there follows (you could underline for emphasis), "I will . . . I will . . . I will . . . I will . . . I will . . . the LORD will . . . the LORD will . . . I will . . . ." God *will* step in and direct developments. Chapter 14 informs us how terrible it will be for the Israelis before the Lord appears, and then "the LORD will go out and fight against those nations, as he fights in the day of battle" (14:3). He will intervene—in Person.

Figures of speech describe what happens next. "I am going to make Jerusalem a cup that sends all the surrounding peoples reeling" (12:2). In other words, their minds will be confused, as if they were intoxicated. "I will make Jerusalem an immovable rock" (12:3). The rest of the verse is a polite translation that should read more literally, "Anybody who tries to budge that rock will get a hernia."[14] Then, "I will strike every horse with panic and its rider with madness. . . . I will blind all the horses of the nations" (12:4). These are ancient figures of warfare. Perhaps we can take the literary license to imagine the modern military machines that besiege Jerusalem being thrown into confusion. "I will make the leaders of Judah like a firepot in a woodpile. . . . They will consume right and left all the surrounding peoples" (12:6). That sparkles like great country preaching! The Israelis will turn on their attackers in great force. "The LORD will shield those who live in Jerusalem . . . [and] will set out to destroy all the nations that attack Jerusalem" (12:8-9).

Perhaps it is best to read this as a picture of God at work on behalf of His people. In John's Revelation, we are given a drama on two stages, with pictures of frightening developments on earth and the counterpoint of strong, confident, history-shaping direction from heaven. Here too we must see more than the battle. We must see the Lord. Go over it again and look for the Lord in it. "I will keep a watchful eye over the house of Judah" (Zechariah 12:4). This is Aaron's benediction fulfilled, the Lord blessing and keeping, the Lord making His face to shine upon them, the Lord turning His full attention toward them (see Numbers 6:24-26). "The leaders of Judah will say in their hearts, 'The people of Jerusalem are strong, because the LORD Almighty is their God.' "

What a phenomenon! What they have today is a strong tradition, some even hold to a religious tradition, together they may share a sense of destiny, but they do not have a sense of God. If anything, their religious differences are their sharpest division. However, when He intervenes, it will be so clear that the leaders will look around and say, "God is among us." An amazing thing!

"On that day I will make the leaders of Judah like a firepot in a woodpile. . . . The feeblest among them will be like David [meaning vigorous and strong], the house of David will be like God, like the Angel of the LORD going before them" (12:6, 8). What a tremendous transformation in their leaders and in their fortunes! "On that day," it says. That phrase occurs fifteen times in these three chapters. No doubt it will be an incredible day when God comes to Israel again with a personal and visible intervention.

A Spirit of Grace and Supplication (12:10-14)

God's intervention will also reach to a deeper level. "And I will pour out on the house of David and the inhabitants of Jerusalem a spirit of grace and supplication" (12:10).

Sometimes praying is like walking through a swamp and we feel like we have accomplished a great feat when we successfully reach the other side. Other times we don't even get started. Then there are those occasions when prayer just flows with "the spirit of supplication."

The spirit of supplication comes to me most frequently in the night, when I am awakened by the Holy Spirit and my soul is free from all that crowds me during the day. Sometimes it is the gift of a specifically focused burden. Other times it is the racing excitement of unusual contact with the throne without any sense of time. It is a tremendous unburdening, with a freedom from the Lord to leave the burdens with Him. The spirit of supplication is an intense form of prayer, not a learned spiritual exercise, but a gift.

The Jewish people have not had a spirit of supplication since the revival at the Water Gate led by Ezra 450 years before Christ (Nehemiah 8-10). But "they will look on me," it says in Zechariah, "the one they have pierced" (12:10). The Messiah's intervention will be dramatic, personal and visible, and they will recognize Him. They will recognize the scars on His hands.

Jewish commentators have had trouble with this text. In the Babylonian Talmud, which was written in the first centuries of the common era, the Rabbis postulated two Messiahs: one who came to suffer and one who came to conquer.[15] Instead, it should be clear that what we have here is that the Messiah will come twice, first to suffer and then to conquer. The first time He came, they detested Him, selling Him for thirty pieces of silver. When He comes again, they will see Him, they will recognize Him as "the one they have pierced," and the Lord will give them all "a spirit of grace and supplication." This time He will not be met with resistance. Instead, their hearts will turn upward and their mourning will be "as one mourns for an only child, and [they will] grieve bitterly for him as one grieves for a firstborn son" (12:10).

The funeral of a child is a wrenching experience. What a metaphor! He also said it will be "like the weeping of Hadad Rimmon in the plain of Megiddo" (12:11). This is a reference to the story of Josiah's death. He was a well-loved young king who saw revival come to his land just years before the Babylonian captivity. There was a cleansing of the temple. They rediscovered the law of God. Because of his conviction that God was with them, Josiah decided to go into battle against their superpower neighbor, and in the gap of Megiddo, on his thirty-ninth birthday, Josiah lost the battle with Pharaoh Neco, he lost his whole army and he lost his life. The nation grieved because their hope for renewal died that day (2 Chronicles 35:20-24).[16] They were affected much like we were by John Kennedy's assassination.

With that comparison, the oracle now says that when these people see Jesus, the Lord in human flesh, come to rescue them from the surrounding international forces, and when they recognize what they have done to Him, there is going to be grief that is as deep as grief for a lost child or as deep as the nation's loss of Josiah. They will all mourn for what they have done: the royal family and the family of the prophet, the family of the priest and the family of the scribe. It will be public mourning, represented by these leaders, and it will be private grief, shared by their families. The land itself will mourn, it says. The prophet foresees a very deep-felt, dramatic turning to the Lord in great remorse for rejecting Jesus as their Shepherd (chapter 11) and for piercing Him (chapter 12).

A Cleansing Fountain (13:1-6)

In addition to intervening in Israel's history and bringing a spirit of grace and supplication, God also comes with a cleansing fountain. "On that day a fountain will be opened to the house of David and the inhabitants of Jerusalem, to cleanse them from sin and impurity" (13:1). Familiar lines in First John extend this figure: "If we confess our sins, he is faithful and just and will forgive us our sins and purify [cleanse] us from all unrighteousness. . . . The blood of Jesus, his Son, purifies [cleanses] us from all sin" (1: 9, 7). It is generally considered somewhat inelegant and primitive to talk about the blood of Christ. We are afraid that the folks on the outside will think we are not very sophisticated if they discover at the heart of our religion is sacrifice and blood. But the picture in Zechariah is a fountain that cleanses from sin, and First John makes known that the fountain is the blood of Jesus.

This is more than merely forgiveness. The more thorough work of God being promised here is cleansing, which we know is harder to accomplish. How often do we ask for forgiveness only to fall back into the same sin? We know that there is something inside of us that needs to be cleansed. Beyond that, our frustration mounts to despair when we sense sin endemic in our church and in our culture, defying our best attempts to change things. Cleansing is a work of God, and it is a thorough work. We celebrate it and renew it every time we lay out the Lord's table of communion.

The cleansing predicted here is specific. First, "I will banish the names of the idols from the land, and they will be remembered no more" (13:2). Walter Kaiser's observation here is helpful: "To 'cut off the names of the idols' [KJV] was equivalent to destroying the idols and everything that suggested that they'd ever existed."[17] It seems idolatry and false prophecy will be major problems, a prediction reinforced by New Testament prophecy (Matthew 24:4-5, 11, 15, 23-24; 2 Thessalonians 2:2-4; Revelation 9:20; 13:4-15).

Our idols are secular, perhaps more subtle because they do not have physical forms. We live for comfort, for what feels good, for prosperity, for success. We live for self-esteem and self-fulfillment. Of course when we see these things in extremes, either in broad, God-careless trends or in someone who is really off-track, we can easily condemn him or her. It is easier to see self-serving in other people than it is to see it in ourselves. But let's admit that we are all vulnerable to the impulses of these modern Western secular idols. We serve whatever gets us what we want.

The Lord tells His chosen people that a day is coming when He will remove from their land the impulse to serve idols of any kind, whether national or personal, whether blatant or subtle. And He is especially determined to remove the "prophets" of that day who promote these alternatives.

Second, God "will remove . . . the spirit of impurity" (13:2). Why is it that we are so prone to flirt with immorality? Our fascination with sin is most obvious in our entertainment. Whether or not we get into it, we certainly are fascinated with it! We like to watch it. We enjoy the titillation of watching other people in sin. Why is that? Would it help us to stop if we visualized a demonic force behind it, a spirit of impurity? On that day, the Lord will remove the spirit of impurity.

The backlash will be terrific, as the following verses show. The parents of those who persist in promoting sin will be so angry that they will murder their own children. There is a precedent for that. Have you ever wondered how anyone could have been so philistine as to deface the magnificent ancient Greek marble statuary that has come down to us with arms smashed and noses missing? The beautiful figures of Aphrodite or Venus are defaced, with breasts broken off. They were destroyed, not by the barbarians that came over the wall from the north, but by Christians. They trashed everything left from that Greek/Roman culture that was so strongly sensual. We may say in our cool detachment that they should have been more careful to recognize art and beauty. But after three centuries of trying to live holy lives in a sex-saturated society, the backlash was overwhelming.[18] When the spirit of impurity is finally lifted and people recognize what an influence it has been on them all, the response is going to be tremendous.

The third cleansing action prophesied here is the removal of false prophets, those who "have told lies in the LORD's name" (13:3).

When Jesus described the entry process at the gate of heaven, He said, "Many will say to me on that day, 'Lord, Lord, did we not prophesy in your name, and in your name drive out demons and perform many miracles?' Then I will tell them plainly, 'I never knew you. Away from me, you evildoers!' " (Matthew 7:22-23). The prophets rejected by Jesus in this picture of the judgment are among those mentioned by Zechariah.

These lying prophets will be embarrassed about the scars on their bodies! Picture the "ecstatic prophets" of Baal when Elijah met them in the great fire-from-heaven challenge on Mount Carmel. They cut themselves until their blood flowed, while Elijah dripped with only sarcasm (1 Kings 18:27-28). The scars on their bodies were marks of their superior spiritual devotion. But "on that day every prophet will be ashamed of his prophetic vision. He will not put on a prophet's garment of hair in order to deceive. He will say, 'I am not a prophet. I am a farmer; the land has been my livelihood since my youth' " (Zechariah 13:4-5). Those who once preened themselves and professed superior spirituality will then seek to disappear in the crowd. And if one is recognized, he will lie about his past and about the scars it left, preferring to be thought a drunken brawler than a purveyor of alternate spiritualities.

It is sobering to consider what the prophets of the Jews have told them over all these years. Their adaptations to host cultures in many different communities of their Diaspora have given the Jewish people a colorful mosaic of widely varied pieties and traditions. But they have also known experiences of binding legalism, thought-controlling leadership, spirit-suppressing fatalism and fanatical resistance to modernity. Many have sought to escape this by embracing the modern, and a tradition of faith has yielded to a cynical secularism that no longer considers adherence to their unique religion to be the defining identity for the Jew. All of these currents have their prophetic voices. But this prophecy of Zechariah clearly predicts that when they look on the One they have pierced, when He intervenes as their Savior again, they will fiercely reject all of their prophetic traditions and receive from the Lord the cleansing work of His fountain for their hearts, their spirits and their minds.

So God comes to Israel again. He intervenes at the darkest hour in their history. He shows Himself to them again and they are thrown into tremendous grief and mourning. He gives them a new impulse to seek Him, and He "opens a fountain" to cleanse them. It is as if the fountain was there, but it had been blocked up like Isaac's wells. Something was in the works. Picture it now suddenly unplugged, spewing out the cleansing stream with startling force. On that day, the Lord will come to His people Israel again.

* * *

We have just looked at a description of future developments for Israel. But the blessings God promises to bring to them when He comes are currently available to us when we seek Him.

First, some of us are besieged by difficulties beyond our ability to endure, and like the Israeli people, we will be overcome if the Lord does not intervene. The encouragement in Zechariah 12:1 is for us too. The Lord who stretches out the heavens and lays the foundations of the earth has created life within us. No matter how far we have fallen, no matter how heinous our sins, there is still hope. The Jewish people have rejected their Good Shepherd but the story is not yet finished. God made a promise to Abraham and He intends to keep it. He will intervene in their history again. Our story is not finished either. He will intervene again for us too. So "let us then approach the throne of grace with confidence, so that we may receive mercy and find grace to help us in our time of need" (Hebrews 4:16).

Second, let's ask the Lord to give us a spirit of supplication. We need Him to give us a new, strong, compelling impulse to seek Him. If He does not give us that we are lost—and we are not naturally inclined to want to be found. Jesus told those who liked His gift of bread but did not like His Bread-of-Life analogy that they did not come to Him because the Father had not given them that urge. "No one can come to me," He said, "unless the Father who sent me draws him" (John 6:44). Even our spiritual hunger is one of God's special gifts.

We need to see Him as the one *we* have pierced. We cannot hold the Jews responsible for His crucifixion. It is our sins that pierced Him. When we see Him visibly, we too will be overcome with grief, because we will recognize, perhaps for the first time, that we drove the nails that pierced His hands. He died for our sins.

We need not wait until that day to face our Lord and to face our sins and deal with them. Let's ask Him for the gift of godly grief to help us to recognize our sins. Let's ask the Lord for a spirit of supplication.

Third, let's ask Him for a gushing fountain of cleansing to wash through our souls and through our churches and through our nation. And don't we need it? Let's ask Him to cleanse us from sin and impurity, to banish the idols from our land and from our hearts, to remove the spirit of impurity and the prophets whose voices only confuse us and lead us astray. Look at what the Lord has promised to do for His chosen people Israel when He comes to them again. Let's ask Him to do it for us too.

When I saw the cleansing fountain
   Open wide for all my sin,
I obeyed the Spirit's wooing
   When He said, "Wilt thou be clean?"
I will praise Him! I will praise Him!
   Praise the Lamb for sinners slain!
Give Him glory, all ye people,
   For His blood can wash away each stain.[19]

Discussion Questions for Further Study

1. What is your attitude toward the end times? Are you fascinated by every detail, perhaps not cautious enough to sort it all out? Or are you on the "overdosed" side, somewhat cynical about it all? Where do you want to be?
2. Read Matthew 24:14 again. What difference does it make that we can see the end from here? What are you doing to take the gospel to "all peoples"?
3. Identify several events in modern Israel that are evidence of the Lord's intervention on behalf of His people.
4. In what areas of your life do you require the "cleansing fountain" that the Lord promised? Where is that fountain required in our country and culture?
5. In what areas of your life do you need a stronger hunger for grace? How would a "spirit of supplication" change your life?

Endnotes

[1] J. Dwight Pentecost, "A Christian Perspective," *Kindred Spirit*, Summer 1988, 3.

[2] John F. Walvoord, *The Nations in Prophecy* (Grand Rapids, MI: Zondervan, 1967), 15.

[3] Timothy C. Morgan, "From One City to the World," *Christianity Today*, April 24, 1995, 36.
[4] Rick Wood, "GCOWE '95—A Major Step Forward in Building a Movement to the Frontiers," *Mission Frontiers*, July-August 1995, 10.
[5] Ibid., 11, quoting Ralph Winter.
[6] Ibid., 12.
[7] *Missions Frontiers,* January-February 1996, 5.
[8] Ibid., 12.
[9] Lance Lambert seeks to document the hand of the Lord in preventing the annihilation of Israel in the Yom Kippur War of 1973 in *Israel: A Secret Documentary* (Wheaton, IL: Tyndale House, 1975).
[10] Robert Reich, "Robert Reich Speaks," *Dollars and Sense*, September-October 1995; chapter 12 in his book *The Coming Irrelevance of Corporate Nationality* (New York: A.A. Knopf, 1991), 136-153, articulates his convictions about the importance of national economies being interconnected.
[11] Eduard Shevardnadze, *The Future Belongs to Freedom* (New York: The Free Press, 1991), 45-46.
[12] "An Ever Closer Union," *TIME*, December 23, 1991.
[13] Elisabeth Elliot, *The Furnace of the Lord: Reflections on the Redemption of the Holy City* (Garden City, NY: Doubleday, 1969).
[14] Walter C. Kaiser, Jr. *Micah-Malachi*, The Communicator's Commentary, vol. 21 (Dallas: Word Books, 1992), 401.
[15] Kenneth L. Barker, *Zechariah*, The Expositor's Bible Commentary, vol. 7, Frank E. Gaebelein, ed. (Grand Rapids, MI: Zondervan, 1986), 684.
[16] Kaiser, 407.
[17] Ibid., 410.
[18] Will Durant, *The Age of Faith* (New York: Simon and Schuster, 1950), 76.
[19] Margaret J. Harris, "I Will Praise Him," *Hymns of the Christian Life* (Camp Hill, PA: Christian Publications, Inc., 1978), # 51.

13

The Triumphant Conclusion

Zechariah 13:7-14:21

"Awake, O sword, against my shepherd,
against the man who is close to me!"
declares the LORD Almighty.
"Strike the shepherd,
and the sheep will be scattered,
and I will turn my hand against the little ones.
In the whole land," declares the LORD,
"two-thirds will be struck down and perish;
yet one-third will be left in it.
This third I will bring into the fire;
I will refine them like silver
and test them like gold.
They will call on my name
and I will answer them;
I will say, 'They are my people,'
and they will say, 'The LORD is our God.' "

A day of the LORD is coming when your plunder will be divided among you.

I will gather all the nations to Jerusalem to fight against it; the city will be captured, the houses ran-

sacked, and the women raped. Half of the city will go into exile, but the rest of the people will not be taken from the city.

Then the LORD will go out and fight against those nations, as he fights in the day of battle. On that day his feet will stand on the Mount of Olives, east of Jerusalem, and the Mount of Olives will be split in two from east to west, forming a great valley, with half of the mountain moving north and half moving south. You will flee by my mountain valley, for it will extend to Azel. You will flee as you fled from the earthquake in the days of Uzziah king of Judah. Then the LORD my God will come, and all the holy ones with him.

On that day there will be no light, no cold or frost. It will be a unique day, without daytime or nighttime—a day known to the LORD. When evening comes, there will be light.

On that day living water will flow out from Jerusalem, half to the eastern sea and half to the western sea, in summer and in winter.

The LORD will be king over the whole earth. On that day there will be one LORD, and his name the only name.

The whole land, from Geba to Rimmon, south of Jerusalem, will become like the Arabah. But Jerusalem will be raised up and remain in its place, from the Benjamin Gate to the site of the First Gate, to the Corner Gate, and from the Tower of Hananel to the royal winepresses. It will be inhabited; never again will it be destroyed. Jerusalem will be secure.

This is the plague with which the LORD will strike all the nations that fought against Jerusalem: Their flesh will rot while they are still standing on their feet, their eyes will rot in their sockets, and their tongues will rot in their mouths. On that day men will be stricken by the LORD *with great panic. Each man will seize the hand of another, and they will attack each other. Judah too will fight at Jerusalem. The wealth of all the surrounding nations will be collected—great quantities of gold and silver and clothing. A similar plague will strike the horses and mules, the camels and donkeys, and all the animals in those camps.*

Then the survivors from all the nations that have attacked Jerusalem will go up year after year to worship the King, the LORD *Almighty, and to celebrate the Feast of Tabernacles. If any of the peoples of the earth do not go up to Jerusalem to worship the King, the* LORD *Almighty, they will have no rain. If the Egyptian people do not go up and take part, they will have no rain. The* LORD *will bring on them the plague he inflicts on the nations that do not go up to celebrate the Feast of Tabernacles. This will be the punishment of Egypt and the punishment of all the nations that do not go up to celebrate the Feast of Tabernacles.*

On that day HOLY TO THE LORD *will be inscribed on the bells of the horses, and the cooking pots in the* LORD*'s house will be like the sacred bowls in front of the altar. Every pot in Jerusalem and Judah will be holy to the* LORD *Almighty, and all who come to sacrifice will take some of the pots and cook in them. And on that day there will no longer be a Canaanite in the house of the* LORD *Almighty.*

Zechariah's last message ends on a triumphant note—a victorious conclusion to the final conflict.

The Cathedrals Quartet sings a toe-tapping version of "I've Read the Back of the Book and We Win!" The upbeat music with the exuberant piano have the right tone of celebration. It is important to come to the end of this study with confidence that the dramatic events predicted here are going to end well.

Zechariah's prophecy is presented more thematically than chronologically, and all of the major themes in this section have been introduced earlier. Those strands are now being drawn together so that the message is unmistakable and the conclusion is strong. It is also like an appendix that answers some remaining questions and fills in some color by addressing the following concerns:

1. How can these terrible end-time events be construed as a work of the Lord? (Zechariah 13:7-9)
2. Tell us again about the battle and Israel's victory. (14:1-7)
3. What will be left when the battle is over? (14:8-11)
4. What will happen to those who oppose the Lord? (14:12-19)
5. What will it be like when pure worship is restored? (14:20-21)

How Can These Terrible End-time Events Be Construed as a Work of the Lord? (13:7-9)

Two answers to this question are presented in this poem. First, God is the One who calls for these events. And second, He has a purpose in them.

Notice the first-person language: The shepherd is

"my shepherd . . . the man who is close to me!" (13:7). It is at the Lord's command that the sword comes against the shepherd; it is at His word that the shepherd is struck. He is the One who brings His people into the fire, but He has an overriding purpose in the events that seem so wrong.

To be sure, the religious leaders who manipulated the crowd and all those who called for Jesus' crucifixion are going to have to answer to God for that. The people who drove the nails through His hands are also going to have to answer to God. All who have sinned are going to have to answer to God for the death of Jesus Christ.

But we face here the other side of the paradox of purpose. It was not a tragic development in what could have been a good story. They did not thwart God's intention with their malevolence, and we did not with our sin. Jesus' burning message to the disciples on the road to Emmaus was a challenge "to believe all that the prophets have spoken! Did not the Christ have to suffer . . . ?" (Luke 24:25-26). In Isaiah 53 the figure is inverted so the Servant of the Lord is not the shepherd but the lamb, and in His death He bore our iniquity. "It was the LORD's will to crush him and cause him to suffer . . . [to make] his life a guilt offering" (53:10). A fundamental article of faith for us is acceptance of this purpose in Christ's suffering, in the Lord's striking the shepherd. "He is the atoning sacrifice for our sins, and not only for ours but also for the sins of the whole world" (1 John 2:2). God's purpose was fulfilled.

We are called to another article of faith in the second line of the couplet: "Strike the shepherd, and the sheep will be scattered" (Zechariah 13:7). So the Lord turns His hand against "the little ones," many perish, the rest are purged, and in the last stanza they return to Him. He calls for these hard developments so that in the end they will call on Him again. The apostle Paul, a Jew who became the "apostle to the Gentiles" (Romans 11:13) recognized that "Israel has experienced a hardening in part until the full number of the Gentiles has come in" (11:25). And when the Lord turns His attention back to the Jewish people, "all Israel will be saved" (11:26). He called them out of all the nations to be His own treasured possession, and "as far as election is concerned . . . [the] gifts and his call are irrevocable" (11:28-29). His purpose in calling the Jewish people to be His chosen will be accomplished. In an unusual way that is happening even now. "Because of [the Jews'] transgression, salvation has come to the Gentiles" (11:11). They can no longer bottle it up and keep it for themselves.

God's purpose runs through all of these devastating experiences. This poem is inserted here as a song of encouragement that the Lord's intention will prevail. All of the scattering, striking, perishing and fire that His people experience intentionally culture a purified pursuit and embrace of God. For every ounce of gold that emerges through the crushing and washing and heat processes, tons of less valuable material are left on the slag pile.

The refining prophesied for Israel is a stunning statement. "Two-thirds will be struck down and perish." The third that is left, He says, "I will bring into the fire . . . [to] refine them like silver and test them like gold" (Zechariah 13:9). One-third of the Jewish people lost their lives in the holocaust. That is comparable to 85 million Americans or 10 million Canadians losing their lives in war or genocide. That would leave an indelible imprint on our national consciousness. Is it any wonder that the Jewish people are touchy about threats against them? But this prediction points to yet another major tragedy. And the last lines are as striking as the high casualty rates: The survivors will return to the Lord in renewal of the covenant that they swore at Sinai. "I will say, 'They are my people,' and they will say, 'The LORD is our God' " (13:9).

Jewish evangelism is not among our more fruitful pursuits. Walter Kaiser laments,

> What will it take for Israel—and all the world—to recognize who this Shepherd really is? We can be assured that at least Israel will finally come to her senses, but oh, by what a national blood bath. . . . Would that more Jews and Gentiles would come to the Messiah, even now, before these terrible days must be endured.[1]

But one way or another, God intends to have His people, and one way or another, He intends to purify them. Because He is committed to His children with such severe mercy, I have found myself praying, "Help me Lord to learn my lessons well this semester, because I have discovered I really don't want to repeat this course." He intends to have us, and He intends to have us purified.

From the perspective of the Lord's purpose, we can embrace rather than endure the fearful end-time prophecies such as the harsh words in Ezekiel 22:

This is what the Sovereign LORD says, "Because you have all become dross, I will gather you into Jerusalem. As men gather silver, copper, iron, lead and tin into a furnace to melt it with a fiery blast, so will I gather you in my anger and my wrath and put you inside the city and melt you. I will gather you and I will blow on you with my fiery wrath, and you will be melted inside her. As silver is melted in a furnace, so you will be melted inside her, and you will know that I the LORD have poured out my wrath upon you." (22:19-22)

The prophecy is about the future of Israel, but the principle is applicable to us all. A recent penetrating song offers this reflection on the theme:

There burns a fire with sacred heat,
white hot with holy flame,
And all who dare pass through its blaze
will not emerge the same . . .
Some as bronze, and some as silver,
some as gold, then with great skill,
All are hammered by their suffering
on the anvil of his will.
The refiner's fire
has now become my soul-desire . . .
Purged and cleansed and purified,
that the Lord be glorified.
He is consuming my soul,
refining me, making me whole.
No matter what I may lose,
I choose the refiner's fire.

It took several months of playing that tape in my car before I was ready to yield to the song's message. It took even longer to adopt the second verse as my own:

I'm learning now to trust his touch,
to crave the fire's embrace,
For though my past with sin was etched,
his mercy did erase.
Each time his purging cleanses deeper
I'm not sure that I'll survive.
Yet, his strength in growing deeper
keeps my hungry soul alive.[2]

God can do that in me. He can do that in Israel. He can do that with His whole creation. And He will because He intends to have us purified and restored to Him. We can look into our hearts and recognize that we need His refining fire. In the middle of it we may ask, "How can a righteous God do this?" But in our hearts we know that He can and that He must. In the end, "I will say, 'They are my people,' and they will say, 'The LORD is our God.' "

Tell Us Again about the Battle and Israel's Victory (14:1-7)

We have read Zechariah's prophecies of the great battle for Jerusalem that is to come: "Judah will be besieged" (12:2); "I will defend my house against marauding forces" (9:8); "Then the LORD will appear over them" (9:14).

Now, in chapter 14 we are told, "A day of the LORD is coming . . . ." At this point you could say that man has had his day, and now the Lord will have *His* day. "A day of the LORD is coming when your plunder will be divided among you" (14:1). So complete will be the destruction of the city on that day that the nations will sit down right there to divide up the Israeli assets they have captured.

> "I will gather all the nations to Jerusalem to fight against it; the city will be captured, the houses ransacked, and the women raped. Half of the city will go into exile, but the rest of the people will not be taken from the city" (14:2).
>
> Then the LORD will go out and fight against those nations, as he fights in the day of battle. On that day his feet will stand on the Mount of Olives, east of Jerusalem, and the Mount of Olives will be split in two from east to west, forming a great valley, with half of the mountain moving north and half moving south. You will flee by my mountain valley, for it will extend to Azel. (14:3-5)

The Mount of Olives is 330 feet higher than the temple mount, a great platform for viewing the Old City. But on that day, this viewpoint mountain will be a great obstacle. The siege of the city will be most severe, and no escape routes will be available. But when this final anti-Semitic onslaught is at its worst, the Lord will miraculously split that mountain in half, dividing the Mount of Olives as He once divided the Red Sea, forming a valley running through it from west to east. In fact, there is already a fault line running right under it in that direction.[3] The parting of the Mount of Olives all the way to Azel on the other side will provide the way out. "You will flee as you fled from the earthquake in the days of Uzziah king of Judah" (14:5).

It may be interesting to note that the seventh bowl of judgment in the Revelation is an "earthquake like [none that] has ever occurred since man has been on earth" (16:18). It will be so traumatic that the cities of all the nations will collapse, islands in the ocean will disappear and familiar mountains will be missing. It isn't hard to envision the parting of the Mount of Olives being part of these supernatural events. Zechariah's description continues of cataclysmic phenomena, dramatic changes in the natural order. "It will be a unique day, without normal daytime or nighttime," without normal light (14:6-7). The Lord will physically appear—reappear—on earth, standing on top of the Mount of Olives, the very spot from which He left, just as the angels said He would (Acts 1:10-11).

The best component of the entire scene is this: "Then the LORD my God will come, and all the holy ones with him" (Zechariah 14:5). Zechariah's use of the personal term, "the LORD my God," indicates that he is caught up in the excitement of this message. He had seen the Lord in many scenes of vision and prophetic oracle, but this one is special! Here "the LORD my God" is surrounded by His holy angels and saints when He descends on the Mount of Olives in visible physical form to rescue His people once again. "Amen. Come Lord Jesus" (Revelation 22:20).[4]

What Will Be Left When the Battle Is Over? (14:8-11)

There will be big changes in Israel.

"On that day living water will flow out from Jerusalem, half to the eastern sea and half to the western sea, in summer and in winter" (Zechariah 14:8). There are not many permanent streams in Israel. The Israelites had always been dependent on the gift of rain from the Lord to fill their cisterns each season, tangibly sensing His displeasure when the rain did not come. God was teaching them to trust Him and to walk in obedience. But this provision of life-giving water is different. It is an artesian well springing up in the city itself, with a stream flowing to the Mediterranean and another to the Jordan/Dead Sea Valley. And unlike most streams in that land, this one will not become a wadi, or dry gulch, when the rain stops—it will not be affected by the seasons.

This is more than just a solution to the chronic water supply problems of the area. It is symbolic of paradise regained, recalling Ezekiel's vision of fresh water flowing out of the temple bringing life to the desert (Ezekiel 47:1-12), or John's vision of "the river of the water of life" in the Holy City (Revelation 22:1-2). This is "living water" flowing out from Jerusalem.

"The LORD will be king over the whole earth. On that day there will be one LORD, and his name the only name" (Zechariah 14:9). The Lord will be king. Think about that when you recite the Lord's Prayer and ask that His kingdom come and His will be done, on earth as it is in heaven. He intends to answer that prayer literally. Imagine no more tension between nations. Imagine no more idolatry or false pursuits. How about no more filth on television, no more pervasive evil in society, no more injustice, no more unrighteousness. Everyone will worship the Lord, and there will be no competitors. It will be a new world!

"The whole land, from Geba to Rimmon, south of Jerusalem, will become like the Arabah" (14:10). In other words, the mountainous and desolate regions of Israel will become fruitful farm lands like the Arabah, the Jordan Valley. And "Jerusalem will be raised up and remain in its place, from the Benjamin Gate to the site of the First Gate, to the Corner Gate, and from the Tower of Hananel to the royal winepresses" (14:10). With the cataclysmic changes of the great earthquake, the city will be elevated and the surrounding mountains leveled. I propose we should understand that both literally and symbolically. "It will be inhabited; never again will it be destroyed. Jerusalem will be secure" (14:11).

In fact, each of these lines can be understood both literally and figuratively. What will be left when the battle is over? (1) A new water source . . . a new life source. (2) A new king . . . Jesus will be the only One even recognized. (3) A new topography . . . a new center of the earth. One hundred years ago, London was the center of the earth, as Britannia ruled the waves. After World War I, New York was the center of the earth because of American economic power. After World War II, Washington became the center of the earth when the United States withdrew from its comfortable isolationism and became a major factor in world affairs. There will come a time when Jerusalem will be the center of the earth and Jesus Christ will reign over the entire world from that city. That is what will be left when the battle is over.

What Will Happen to Those Who Oppose the Lord? (14:12-19)

The first answer to this question begins in verse 12:

> This is the plague with which the LORD will strike all the nations that fought against Jerusalem: Their flesh will rot while they are still standing on their feet, their eyes will rot in their sockets, and their tongues will rot in their mouths. On that day men will be stricken by the LORD with great panic. Each man will seize the hand of another, and they will attack each other. Judah too will fight at Jerusalem. The wealth of all the surrounding nations will be collected—great quantities of gold and silver and clothing. A similar plague will strike the horses and mules, the camels and donkeys, and all the animals in those camps. (14:12-15)

Israel's enemies are going to be trapped. This chapter began with the plunder that the nations found in Israel and Jerusalem will be divided among them. But after the Lord's intervention, the wealth left to the surviving Israelites will be enormous. The first answer is that many of those who oppose the Lord will lose their lives hideously in the great battle.

> Then the survivors from all the nations that have attacked Jerusalem will go up year after year to worship the King, the LORD Almighty,

> and to celebrate the Feast of Tabernacles. If any of the peoples of the earth do not go up to Jerusalem to worship the King, the LORD Almighty, they will have no rain. If the Egyptian people do not go up and take part, they will have no rain. (14:16-18)

In fact there is never any rain in Egypt. This may be an implicit promise that this special blessing of God will be available to them too—a dramatic change in climate! There is this extra word of warning for Egypt however: "The LORD will bring on them the plague he inflicts on the nations that do not go up to celebrate the Feast of Tabernacles" (14:18). Egypt was punished once before by great plagues, so this should send a shudder through their national soul. But it will be the unhappy experience of all of the nations that do not go up to celebrate the Feast of Tabernacles. What will happen to those who oppose the Lord? If they survive, they will finally surrender to the Lord. Some may do that willingly. It seems that some will surrender unwillingly. But surrender they shall!

Perhaps it is important to recognize that by this last chapter, the Messiah's identity is totally merged in the identity of the Lord Almighty. The One who comes as their Champion and actually leads them in war is the One who will be King and who will receive their worship. So, Jesus Christ will be worshiped as the Lord Almighty, and those who refuse to come to Jerusalem to give Him that honor will suffer for their rebellion.

There is a curious note in the last chapter of Matthew. Jesus had sent His disciples up to Galilee, to the mountain where He said that He would meet them. He came to them there, and "when they saw him, they worshiped him; but some doubted" (Matthew 28:17). The Lord is so gracious when we have honest doubts. They were doing their best to try to comprehend what was happening, and they were not at all sure, but they worshiped Him. His presence had a numinous power, and their natural instinct was worship. The Jews were strict about not worshiping idols or their leaders as the other nations did. They did not worship angels and they did not worship their prophets or teachers, which is what Jesus had been to them. They fanatically suppressed any worship but that which they gave to the one true God. And when Jesus appeared in His resurrection splendor, they saw Him and they worshiped. Without yet understanding it completely, their sense of their Messiah and their sense of the Lord Almighty was merging. Here in Zechariah 14 the merger is complete. Not only will that identity be seen, it will be demanded. Every knee will bow and every tongue confess that Jesus Christ is Lord (Philippians 2:10-11).

And what about the Feast of Tabernacles? They had several feasts, and I suppose any one of them would have worked here as an illustration of this international phenomenon of shared worship. But the Feast of Tabernacles is an especially good example. The Hebrew people had two Thanksgivings. One was at the beginning of the harvest season. After the first day of reaping the harvest, they would stop the entire harvesting operation to meet the Lord with the worship gift of their firstfruits (Leviticus 23:9). Their second Thanksgiving festival, the Feast of Tabernacles, was at the end of the harvest, celebrating the ingathering (23:34, 39). They celebrated the fact that they were a blessed people.

This Feast of Tabernacles to which Zechariah refers is symbolic of the final ingathering of the nations—all of God's people, Jews and Gentiles, finally worshiping and serving the Lord together.

What Will It Be Like When Pure Worship Is Restored? (14:20-21)

Verses 20 and 21 contain several symbols that would have been familiar to Zechariah's people. The colorful metaphors that would have been clear to them take a little probing and explaining for us to understand. These last verses would be a sweet word to folks who were really tired of living in a world of mixed motives, with so many people of nominal faith.

"On that day HOLY TO THE LORD will be inscribed on the bells of the horses." HOLY TO THE LORD is what was inscribed on the gold plaque on the high priest's turban. He was holy to the Lord, and so was everything that he worked with. Now it is going on the horses' harnesses and on "the cooking pots in the LORD's house," which "will be like the sacred bowls in front of the altar." We have a dim sense of that when we gold plate our communion service and treat the church sanctuary as sacred. Though we are not as careful as they were, we know that our worship should be more than casual or common. But now even the vessels in the church kitchen will be "holy to the Lord." Not only that, "Every pot in Jerusalem and Judah will be holy to the LORD Almighty, and all who come to sacrifice will take some of the pots and cook in them." There will no longer be a distinction between sacred and common vessels, not because everything in the house of the Lord will become common, but because everything in life will be holy to the Lord.

"And on that day there will no longer be a Canaanite in the house of the LORD Almighty" (14:21). "Canaanite" was a slur to describe anyone considered unclean. The Canaanite was the phony, the one who professed piety but lived in blatant sin. Anyone who would stoop to selling merchandise in the temple was a "Canaanite." He or she was a vendor of animals for sacrifice or a money changer or a tax collector who was flagrantly skimming an inordinate profit, a chiseler, a used-car salesman.[5] Can you imagine a world without any of that? That is exactly what we are being asked to expect. In the symbols of their society, we have pictured here holiness in public life—the bells on the horses, holiness in religious life—the cooking pots in the house of the Lord, and holiness in private life—every pot in the whole community. All of life is now holy to the Lord. And that is the last picture left us in this tremendous photo album.

Conclusion

We have worked through some heavy material—heavy because it is difficult literature, hard to understand with unfamiliar allusions and foreign forms. But the content is heavy too. Some people read the prophetic literature in the Bible fearfully. It is important to be realistic, to know what to expect, even if that is uncomfortable. But more than that, it is important to see who is making it all happen. John's vision of the future is a Revelation of Jesus Christ. Zechariah's is a vision of the Lord in control.

Francis Ford Cappola tried to bring the ugly reality of the Vietnam War to those who saw it only through the surrealism of television. His movie, *Apocalypse Now*, has a battle scene in which the main character picks his way carefully through a major firefight. "Do you know who's in charge here?" he asks a frenzied machine gunner. The answer was a strange, wordless stare.[6] The filmmaker's point registers that once war gets started, it has an irrationality all its own, with nobody in charge. But we must be sure to recognize that in this prophecy that is never true. No matter what it looks like from our perspective in the battle, the Lord is always in charge.

From the beginning, the intention of Zechariah's book has been to give us another perspective on what is happening around us. Through the vision scenes of the first several chapters, we see God in control of all that is happening on earth and in heaven. The extended answer to the fasting question shows us that his standard of righteousness is still intact. And the oracles of the last five chapters are a picture of things to come. We need to see all of these things clearly.

Zechariah's name means "Yahweh remembers." His message, from first to last, was that God had not forgotten His people. They may have felt forgotten. Others may have considered them a marginal ethnic group, if they considered them at all. But the Lord had made an unconditional promise to Abraham, which He often confirmed, that they would be His people and that He would bless them. They have to go a long way around to finally come back to what

God intended for them, but all of this is the picture of how He intends to work it out. And in the end, "I will say, 'They are my people,' and they will say, 'The LORD is our God' " (Zechariah 13:9).

The small community of Jews who had returned from Babylon to their own land were not doing very well, and the messages from the Lord through Zechariah were given to help them deal with life in the real world. Like theirs, our lives may be hard, and getting harder, but that is not all there is. We need to see what is important to the Lord, what He is planning and what is already happening behind the scenes. All of this is intended to give us strength and hope. We conclude with the affirmation, "The LORD will be king over the whole earth" (14:9).

Discussion Questions for Further Study

1. How do you feel when you read apocalyptic descriptions of horrible events in the future clearly identified as things that God will bring about? Does it challenge or change your concept of God?
2. What pieces can you see already in place for the great battle described in Zechariah 14:1-7?
3. All of creation is groaning as it waits for the Lord's return (Romans 8:22). List aspects of renewal that you are eager to see when He comes.
4. It certainly is sobering to read about what will happen to those who oppose Christ. Who do you know who is opposed to Him that you are burdened to add to your prayer list?
5. What can we learn from the brief description of pure worship in Zechariah 14:20-21 that can help to renew our present worship?

6. The message of the book from first to last is that the Lord is in control. In what areas of your life would a deeper confidence in Him make a difference?

Endnotes

[1] Walter C. Kaiser, Jr. *Micah-Malachi*, The Communicator's Commentary, vol. 21 (Dallas: Word Books, 1992), 414.

[2] "Refiner's Fire," words and music by John Mohr and Randall Dennis. Birdwing Music/Jonathan Mark Music/JR Dennis Music, 1989.

[3] Kaiser, 420.

[4] Other descriptions of the Lord's return are found in Matthew 25:31-46 and First Thessalonians 4:16-17.

[5] Joyce G. Baldwin, *Haggai, Zechariah, Malachi: An Introduction and Commentary*, The Tyndale Old Testament Commentaries (Downers Grove, IL: InterVarsity, 1972), 208; and Kenneth Barker, *The Expositor's Bible Commentary*, vol. 7 (Grand Rapids, MI: Zondervan Publishing House, 1985), 697.

[6] *Apocalypse Now*, Paramount Pictures, 1979.

Time Line

B.C.	
605	First group of exiles taken to Babylon, including Daniel.
597	Second group of exiles taken to Babylon, including King Jehoiachin and Ezekiel.
586	Nebuchadnezzar destroys Jerusalem.
550	Cyrus the Persian takes over the Median Empire.
539	Babylon falls to the Persians.
538	Cyrus announces new policy of repatriation.
537	Zerubbabel and Joshua lead a return of exiles.
536	Foundation of the Second Temple laid.
530	Cambyses succeeds Cyrus.
522	Cambyses commits suicide.
520, August 29	Haggai's first sermon.
520, September 21	Work on the temple project is resumed.
520, November	Zechariah's "Return to Me" message.
520, December 18	Haggai preaches at the laying of the temple cornerstone.
520, Year End	Darius firmly in control of the Persian Empire.
519, February 15	Zechariah's eight-scene vision.
518, December 7	Group from Bethel inquires about fasting.
516	Dedication of the Second Temple.

Bibliography

Works on Zechariah

Baldwin, Joyce G. *Haggai, Zechariah, Malachi: An Introduction and Commentary,* The Old Testament Commentaries. Downers Grove, IL: InterVarsity, 1972.

Barker, Kenneth. *Daniel, Minor Prophets,* The Expositor's Bible Commentary, vol. 7. Grand Rapids, MI: Zondervan, 1985.

Coggins, R.J. *Haggai, Zechariah, Malachi*. Sheffield: JSOT Press, 1987.

Gaebelein, A.C. *Studies in Zechariah.* New York: "Our Hope" Publication Office, n.d.

Kaiser, Walter C., Jr. *Micah-Malachi*, The Communicator's Commentary, vol. 21. Dallas, TX: Word Books, 1992.

Kail, Carl Friedrich, *The Twelve Minor Prophets*, Biblical Commentary on the Old Testament, vol. 11. Martin, James, translator. Grand Rapids, MI: Eerdmans, 1989.

Leupold, H.C. *Exposition of Zechariah*. Columbus: Wartburg Press, 1956.

McGee, J. Vernon. *Zechariah*. Pasadena: Thru the Bible Books, 1979.

Meyer, F.B. *The Prophet of Hope: Studies in Zechariah*. London: Morgan and Scott, 1900.

Moore, Thomas V. *A Commentary on Zechariah*, The Geneva Series of Commentaries. London: Banner of Truth Trust, 1958.

General Works

Bruce, F.F. *Israel and the Nations*. Grand Rapids, Eerdmans, 1963.

Payne, J. Barton. *Encyclopedia of Biblical Prophecy: The Complete Guide to Scriptural Predictions and Their Fulfillment*. New York: Harper and Row, 1973.

Whiston, William, translator. *The Works of Flavius Josephus.* New York: Buccaneer Books, 1990.